CW00972928

D1711982

SONGS FROM BOOKS

PREFACE

I have collected in this volume practically all the verses and chapter-headings scattered through my books. In several cases where only a few lines of verse were originally used, I have given in full the song, etc., from which they were taken.

RUDYARD KIPLING.

'CITIES AND THRONES AND POWERS'

Cities and Thrones and Powers,
　　Stand in Time's eye,
Almost as long as flowers,
　　Which daily die.
But, as new buds put forth
　　To glad new men,
Out of the spent and unconsidered Earth,
　　The Cities rise again.

This season's Daffodil,
　　She never hears,
What change, what chance, what chill,
　　Cut down last year's:
But with bold countenance,
　　And knowledge small,
Esteems her seven days' continuance
　　To be perpetual.

So Time that is o'er-kind,
　　To all that be,
Ordains us e'en as blind,
　　As bold as she:
That in our very death,
　　And burial sure,
Shadow to shadow, well persuaded, saith,
　　'See how our works endure!'

CONTENTS

THE RECALL

I am the land of their fathers.
In me the virtue stays.
I will bring back my children,
After certain days.

Under their feet in the grasses
My clinging magic runs.
They shall return as strangers,
They shall remain as sons.

Over their heads in the branches
Of their new-bought, ancient trees,
I weave an incantation
And draw them to my knees.

Scent of smoke in the evening.
Smell of rain in the night,
The hours, the days and the seasons,
Order their souls aright;

Till I make plain the meaning
Of all my thousand years—
Till I fill their hearts with knowledge.
While I fill their eyes with tears.

PUCK'S SONG

See you the ferny ride that steals
Into the oak-woods far?
O that was whence they hewed the keels
That rolled to Trafalgar.

And mark you where the ivy clings
To Bayham's mouldering walls?
O there we cast the stout railings
That stand around St. Paul's.

See you the dimpled track that runs
All hollow through the wheat?
O that was where they hauled the guns
That smote King Philip's fleet.

Out of the Weald, the secret Weald,
Men sent in ancient years,
The horse-shoes red at Flodden Field,
The arrows at Poitiers.

See you our little mill that clacks,
So busy by the brook?
She has ground her corn and paid her tax
Ever since Domesday Book.

See you our stilly woods of oak?
And the dread ditch beside?
O that was where the Saxons broke
On the day that Harold died.

See you the windy levels spread
About the gates of Rye?
O that was where the Northmen fled,
When Alfred's ships came by.

See you our pastures wide and lone,
Where the red oxen browse?
O there was a City thronged and known.
Ere London boasted a house.

And see you, after rain, the trace
Of mound and ditch and wall?
O that was a Legion's camping-place,
When Cæsar sailed from Gaul.

And see you marks that show and fade,
Like shadows on the Downs?
O they are the lines the Flint Men made,
To guard their wondrous towns.

Trackway and Camp and City lost,
Salt Marsh where now is corn;
Old Wars, old Peace, old Arts that cease,
And so was England born!

She is not any common Earth,
Water or wood or air,
But Merlin's Isle of Gramarye,
Where you and I will fare.

THE WAY THROUGH THE WOODS

They shut the road through the woods
Seventy years ago.
Weather and rain have undone it again,
And now you would never know
There was once a road through the woods
Before they planted the trees.
It is underneath the coppice and heath,
And the thin anemones.
Only the keeper sees
That, where the ring-dove broods,
And the badgers roll at ease,
There was once a road through the woods.

Yet, if you enter the woods
Of a summer evening late,
When the night-air cools on the trout-ringed pools
Where the otter whistles his mate.
(They fear not men in the woods.
Because they see so few)
You will hear the beat of a horse's feet,
And the swish of a skirt in the dew,
Steadily cantering through
The misty solitudes,
As though they perfectly knew
The old lost road through the woods . . .
But there is no road through the woods!

A THREE-PART SONG

I'm just in love with all these three,
The Weald and the Marsh and the Down countrie;
Nor I don't know which I love the most,
The Weald or the Marsh or the white chalk coast!

I've buried my heart in a ferny hill,
Twix' a liddle low shaw an' a great high gill.
Oh hop-bine yaller an' wood-smoke blue,
I reckon you'll keep her middling true!

I've loosed my mind for to out and run
On a Marsh that was old when Kings begun.
Oh Romney Level and Brenzett reeds,
I reckon you know what my mind needs!

I've given my soul to the Southdown grass,
And sheep-bells tinkled where you pass.
Oh Firle an' Ditchling an' sails at sea,
I reckon you keep my soul for me!

THE RUN OF THE DOWNS

The Weald is good, the Downs are best—
I'll give you the run of 'em, East to West.
Beachy Head and Winddoor Hill,
They were once and they are still,
Firle, Mount Caburn and Mount Harry
Go back as far as sums'll carry.
Ditchling Beacon and Chanctonbury Ring,
They have looked on many a thing,
And what those two have missed between 'em
I reckon Truleigh Hill has seen 'em.
Highden, Bignor and Duncton Down
Knew Old England before the Crown.
Linch Down, Treyford and Sunwood
Knew Old England before the Flood.
And when you end on the Hampshire side—
Butser's old as Time and Tide.
The Downs are sheep, the Weald is corn,
You be glad you are Sussex born!

BROOKLAND ROAD

I was very well pleased with what I knowed,
I reckoned myself no fool—
Till I met with a maid on the Brookland Road,
That turned me back to school.

    Low down—low down!
    Where the liddle green lanterns shine—
    O maids, I've done with 'ee all but one,
    And she can never be mine!

'Twas right in the middest of a hot June night,
With thunder duntin' round,
And I see'd her face by the fairy light
That beats from off the ground.

She only smiled and she never spoke,
She smiled and went away;
But when she'd gone my heart was broke,
And my wits was clean astray.

O stop your ringing and let me be—
Let be, O Brookland bells!
You'll ring Old Goodman[1] out of the sea,
Before I wed one else!

---

1 Earl Godwin of the Goodwin Sands?

Old Goodman's Farm is rank sea-sand,
And was this thousand year:
But it shall turn to rich plough land
Before I change my dear.

O, Fairfield Church is water-bound
From autumn to the spring;
But it shall turn to high hill ground
Before my bells do ring.

O, leave me walk on the Brookland Road,
In the thunder and warm rain—
O, leave me look where my love goed,
And p'raps I'll see her again!

> *Low down—low down!*
> *Where the liddle green lanterns shine—*
> *O maids, I've done with 'ee all but one,*
> *And she can never be mine!*

THE SACK OF THE GODS

Strangers drawn from the ends of the earth, jewelled and plumed were
    we.
I was Lord of the Inca race, and she was Queen of the Sea.
Under the stars beyond our stars where the new-forged meteors glow
Hotly we stormed Valhalla, a million years ago.

Ever'neath high Valhalla Hall the well-tuned horns begin
When the swords are out in the underworld, and the weary Gods come in.
Ever through high Valhalla Gate the Patient Angel goes;
He opens the eyes that are blind with hate—he joins the hands of foes.

Dust of the stars was under our feet, glitter of stars above—
Wrecks of our wrath dropped reeling down as we fought and we spurned
    and we strove.
Worlds upon worlds we tossed aside, and scattered them to and fro,
The night that we stormed Valhalla, a million years ago!

They are forgiven as they forgive all those dark wounds and deep,
Their beds are made on the lap of Time and they lie down and sleep.
They are forgiven as they forgive all those old wounds that bleed,
They shut their eyes from their worshippers. They sleep till the world has need.

She with the star I had marked for my own—I with my set desire—
Lost in the loom of the Night of Nights—lighted by worlds afire—
Met in a war against the Gods where the headlong meteors glow,
Hewing our way to Valhalla, a million years ago!

They will come back—come back again, as long as the red Earth rolls.
He never wasted a leaf or a tree. Do you think He would squander souls?

THE KINGDOM

Now we are come to our Kingdom,
And the State is thus and thus;
Our legions wait at the Palace gate—
Little it profits us,
Now we are come to our Kingdom!

Now we are come to our Kingdom,
And the Crown is ours to take—
With a naked sword at the Council board,
And under the throne the Snake,
Now we are come to our Kingdom!

Now we are come to our Kingdom,
And the Realm is ours by right,
With shame and fear for our daily cheer,
And heaviness at night,
Now we are come to our Kingdom!

Now we are come to our Kingdom,
But my love's eyelids fall.
All that I wrought for, all that I fought for,
Delight her nothing at all.
My crown is of withered leaves,
For she sits in the dust and grieves.
Now we are come to our Kingdom!

26

TARRANT MOSS

I closed and drew for my love's sake
That now is false to me,
And I slew the Reiver of Tarrant Moss
And set Dumeny free.

They have gone down, they have gone down,
They are standing all arow—
Twenty knights in the peat-water,
That never struck a blow!

Their armour shall not dull nor rust,
Their flesh shall not decay,
For Tarrant Moss holds them in trust,
Until the Judgment Day.

Their soul went from them in their youth,
Ah God, that mine had gone,
Whenas I leaned on my love's truth
And not on my sword alone!

Whenas I leaned on lad's belief
And not on my naked blade—
And I slew a thief, and an honest thief,
For the sake of a worthless maid.

They have laid the Reiver low in his place,
They have set me up on high,
But the twenty knights in the peat-water
Are luckier than I.

And ever they give me gold and praise
And ever I mourn my loss—
For I struck the blow for my false love's sake
And not for the Men of the Moss!

SIR RICHARD'S SONG

(A.D. 1066)

I followed my Duke ere I was a lover,
    To take from England fief and fee;
But now this game is the other way over—
    But now England hath taken me!

I had my horse, my shield and banner,
    And a boy's heart, so whole and free;
But now I sing in another manner—
    But now England hath taken me!

As for my Father in his tower,
    Asking news of my ship at sea;
He will remember his own hour—
    Tell him England hath taken me!

As for my Mother in her bower,
    That rules my Father so cunningly,
She will remember a maiden's power—
    Tell her England hath taken me!

As for my Brother in Rouen City,
　　A nimble and naughty page is he,
But he will come to suffer and pity—
　　Tell him England hath taken me!

As for my little Sister waiting
　　In the pleasant orchards of Normandie,
Tell her youth is the time for mating—
　　Tell her England hath taken me!

As for my Comrades in camp and highway,
　　That lift their eyebrows scornfully,
Tell them their way is not my way—
　　Tell them England hath taken me!

Kings and Princes and Barons famèd,
　　Knights and Captains in your degree;
Hear me a little before I am blamèd—
　　Seeing England hath taken me!

Howso great man's strength be reckoned,
　　There are two things he cannot flee;
Love is the first, and Death is the second—
　　And Love in England hath taken me!

A TREE SONG

(A.D. 1200)

Of all the trees that grow so fair,
  Old England to adorn,
Greater are none beneath the Sun,
  Than Oak, and Ash, and Thorn.
Sing Oak, and Ash, and Thorn, good sirs
  (All of a Midsummer morn)!
Surely we sing no little thing,
  In Oak, and Ash, and Thorn!

Oak of the Clay lived many a day
  Or ever Æneas began;
Ash of the Loam was a lady at home
  When Brut was an outlaw man.
Thorn of the Down saw New Troy Town
  (From which was London born);
Witness hereby the ancientry
  Of Oak, and Ash, and Thorn!

Yew that is old in churchyard mould,
  He breedeth a mighty bow;
Alder for shoes do wise men choose,
  And beech for cups also.

But when ye have killed, and your bowl is spilled,
    And your shoes are clean outworn,
Back ye must speed for all that ye need,
    To Oak, and Ash, and Thorn!

Ellum she hateth mankind, and waiteth
    Till every gust be laid,
To drop a limb on the head of him
    That anyway trusts her shade:
But whether a lad be sober or sad,
    Or mellow with ale from the horn,
He will take no wrong when he lieth along
    'Neath Oak, and Ash, and Thorn!

Oh, do not tell the Priest our plight,
    Or he would call it a sin;
But—we have been out in the woods all night,
    A-conjuring Summer in!

And we bring you news by word of mouth—
    Good news for cattle and corn—
Now is the Sun come up from the South,
    With Oak, and Ash, and Thorn!

Sing Oak, and Ash, and Thorn, good sirs
    (All of a Midsummer morn)!
England shall bide till Judgment Tide,
    By Oak, and Ash, and Thorn!

CUCKOO SONG

Spring begins in Southern England on the 14th April, on which date the Old Woman lets the Cuckoo out of her basket at Heathfield Fair—locally known as Heffle Cuckoo Fair.

Tell it to the locked-up trees,
Cuckoo, bring your song here!
Warrant, Act and Summons, please.
For Spring to pass along here!
Tell old Winter, if he doubt,
Tell him squat and square—a!
Old Woman!
Old Woman!
Old Woman's let the Cuckoo out
At Heffle Cuckoo Fair—a!

March has searched and April tried—
'Tisn't long to May now,
Not so far to Whitsuntide,
And Cuckoo's come to stay now!
Hear the valiant fellow shout
Down the orchard bare—a!
Old Woman!
Old Woman!
Old Woman's let the Cuckoo out
At Heffle Cuckoo Fair—a!

When your heart is young and gay
And the season rules it—
Work your works and play your play
'Fore the Autumn cools it!
Kiss you turn and turn about,
But my lad, beware—a!
Old Woman!
Old Woman!
Old Woman's let the Cuckoo out
At Heffle Cuckoo Fair—a!

A CHARM

Take of English earth as much
As either hand may rightly clutch.
In the taking of it breathe
Prayer for all who lie beneath.
Not the great nor well-bespoke,
But the mere uncounted folk
Of whose life and death is none
Report or lamentation.
    Lay that earth upon thy heart,
    And thy sickness shall depart!

It shall sweeten and make whole
Fevered breath and festered soul.
It shall mightily restrain
Over-busy hand and brain.
It shall ease thy mortal strife
'Gainst the immortal woe of life,
Till thyself restored shall prove
By what grace the Heavens do move.

Take of English flowers these—
Spring's full-facèd primroses,
Summer's wild wide-hearted rose,
Autumn's wall-flower of the close,
And, thy darkness to illume,

Winter's bee-thronged ivy-bloom.
Seek and serve them where they bide
From Candlemas to Christmas-tide,
    For these simples, used aright,
    Can restore a failing sight.

These shall cleanse and purify
Webbed and inward-turning eye;
These shall show thee treasure hid,
Thy familiar fields amid;
And reveal (which is thy need)
Every man a King indeed!

THE PRAIRIE

'I see the grass shake in the sun for leagues on either hand,
I see a river loop and run about a treeless land—
An empty plain, a steely pond, a distance diamond-clear,
And low blue naked hills beyond. And what is that to fear?'

'Go softly by that river-side or, when you would depart,
You'll find its every winding tied and knotted round your heart.
Be wary as the seasons pass, or you may ne'er outrun
The wind that sets that yellowed grass a-shiver 'neath the Sun.'

'I hear the summer storm outblown—the drip of the grateful wheat.
I hear the hard trail telephone a far-off horse's feet.
I hear the horns of Autumn blow to the wild-fowl overhead;
And I hear the hush before the snow. And what is that to dread?'

'Take heed what spell the lightning weaves—what charm the echoes
    shape—
Or, bound among a million sheaves, your soul may not escape.
Bar home the door of summer nights lest those high planets drown
The memory of near delights in all the longed-for town.'

'What need have I to long or fear? Now, friendly, I behold
My faithful seasons robe the year in silver and in gold.
Now I possess and am possessed of the land where I would be,
And the curve of half Earth's generous breast shall soothe and ravish me!'

CHAPTER HEADINGS

PLAIN TALES FROM THE HILLS

Look, you have cast out Love! What Gods are these
You bid me please?
The Three in One, the One in Three? Not so!
To my own Gods I go.
It may be they shall give me greater ease
Than your cold Christ and tangled Trinities.

> *Lispeth.*

When the Earth was sick and the Skies were grey,
And the woods were rotted with rain,
The Dead Man rode through the autumn day
To visit his love again.

His love she neither saw nor heard,
So heavy was her shame;
And tho' the babe within her stirred
She knew not that he came.

> *The Other Man.*

Cry 'Murder' in the market-place, and each
Will turn upon his neighbour anxious eyes
Asking;—'Art thou the man?' We hunted Cain

Some centuries ago across the world.
This bred the fear our own misdeeds maintain
Today.

His Wedded Wife.

Go, stalk the red deer o'er the heather,
Ride, follow the fox if you can!
But, for pleasure and profit together,
Allow me the hunting of Man—
The chase of the Human, the search for the Soul
To its ruin—the hunting of Man.

Pig.

'Stopped in the straight when the race was his own!
Look at him cutting it—cur to the bone!'
Ask ere the youngster be rated and chidden
What did he carry and how was he ridden?
Maybe they used him too much at the start;
Maybe Fate's weight-cloths are breaking his heart.

In the Pride of his Youth.

'And some are sulky, while some will plunge.
(So ho! Steady! Stand still, you!)
Some you must gentle, and some you must lunge.
(There! There! Who wants to kill you?)
Some—there are losses in every trade—
Will break their hearts ere bitted and made,
Will fight like fiends as the rope cuts hard,
And die dumb-mad in the breaking-yard.'

Thrown Away.

The World hath set its heavy yoke
Upon the old white-bearded folk
Who strive to please the King.
God's mercy is upon the young,
God's wisdom in the baby tongue
That fears not anything.

Tod's Amendment.

Not though you die tonight, O Sweet, and wail,
A spectre at my door,
Shall mortal Fear make Love immortal fail—
I shall but love you more,
Who, from Death's House returning, give me still
One moment's comfort in my matchless ill.

By Word of Mouth.

They burnt a corpse upon the sand—
The light shone out afar;
It guided home the plunging boats
That beat from Zanzibar.
Spirit of Fire, where'er Thy altars rise,
Thou art the Light of Guidance to our eyes!

In Error.

Ride with an idle whip, ride with an unused heel.
But, once in a way, there will come a day

When the colt must be taught to feel
The lash that falls, and the curb that galls, and the sting of the rowelled
    steel.

    The Conversion of Aurelian McGoggin.

It was not in the open fight
We threw away the sword,
But in the lonely watching
In the darkness by the ford.
The waters lapped, the night-wind blew,
Full-armed the Fear was born and grew,
From panic in the night.

    The Rout of the White Hussars.

In the daytime, when she moved about me,
In the night, when she was sleeping at my side,—
I was wearied, I was wearied of her presence.
Day by day and night by night I grew to hate her—
Would God that she or I had died!

    The Bronckhorst Divorce Case.

A stone's throw out on either hand
From that well-ordered road we tread,
And all the world is wild and strange;
Churel and ghoul and Djinn and sprite
Shall bear us company tonight,
For we have reached the Oldest Land
Wherein the powers of Darkness range.

In the House of Suddhoo.

Tonight, God knows what thing shall tide,
The Earth is racked and fain—
Expectant, sleepless, open-eyed;
And we, who from the Earth were made,
Thrill with our Mother's pain.

False Dawn.

Pit where the buffalo cooled his hide,
By the hot sun emptied, and blistered and dried;
Log in the reh-grass, hidden and lone;
Bund where the earth-rat's mounds are strown;
Cave in the bank where the sly stream steals;
Aloe that stabs at the belly and heels,
Jump if you dare on a steed untried—
Safer it is to go wide—go wide!
Hark, from in front where the best men ride;—
'Pull to the off, boys! Wide! Go wide!'

Cupid's Arrows.

He drank strong waters and his speech was coarse;
He purchased raiment and forbore to pay;
He stuck a trusting junior with a horse,
And won gymkhanas in a doubtful way.
Then, 'twixt a vice and folly, turned aside
To do good deeds and straight to cloak them, lied.

A Bank Fraud.

42

COLD IRON

'Gold is for the mistress—silver for the maid—
Copper for the craftsman cunning at his trade.'
'Good!' said the Baron, sitting in his hall,
'But Iron—Cold Iron—is master of them all.'

So he made rebellion 'gainst the King his liege,
Camped before his citadel and summoned it to siege.
'Nay!' said the cannoneer on the castle wall,
'But Iron—Cold Iron—shall be master of you all!'

Woe for the Baron and his knights so strong,
When the cruel cannon-balls laid 'em all along!
He was taken prisoner, he was cast in thrall,
And Iron—Cold Iron—was master of it all.

Yet his King spake kindly (Ah, how kind a Lord!)
'What if I release thee now and give thee back thy sword?'
'Nay!' said the Baron, 'mock not at my fall,
For Iron—Cold Iron—is master of men all.'

'Tears are for the craven, prayers are for the clown—
Halters for the silly neck that cannot keep a crown.'
'As my loss is grievous, so my hope is small,
For Iron—Cold Iron—must be master of men all!'

Yet his King made answer (few such Kings there be!)
'Here is Bread and here is Wine—sit and sup with me.
Eat and drink in Mary's Name, the whiles I do recall
How Iron—Cold Iron—can be master of men all!'

He took the Wine and blessed It. He blessed and brake the Bread.
With His own Hands He served Them, and presently He said:
'See! These Hands they pierced with nails, outside My city wall,
Show Iron—Cold Iron—to be master of men all!

'Wounds are for the desperate, blows are for the strong,
Balm and oil for weary hearts all cut and bruised with wrong.
I forgive thy treason—I redeem thy fall—
For Iron—Cold Iron—must be master of men all!'

'Crowns are for the valiant—sceptres for the bold!
Thrones and powers for mighty men who dare to take and hold.'
'Nay!' said the Baron, kneeling in his hall,
'But Iron—Cold Iron—is master of man all!
Iron out of Calvary is master of men all!'

A SONG OF KABIR

Oh, light was the world that he weighed in his hands!
Oh, heavy the tale of his fiefs and his lands!
He has gone from the *guddee* and put on the shroud,
And departed in guise of *bairagi* avowed!

Now the white road to Delhi is mat for his feet.
The *sal* and the *kikar* must guard him from heat.
His home is the camp, and the waste, and the crowd—
He is seeking the Way as *bairagi* avowed!

He has looked upon Man, and his eyeballs are clear—
(There was One; there is One, and but One, saith Kabir);
The Red Mist of Doing has thinned to a cloud—
He has taken the Path for *bairagi* avowed!

To learn and discern of his brother the clod,
Of his brother the brute, and his brother the God,
He has gone from the council and put on the shroud
('Can ye hear?' saith Kabir), a *bairagi* avowed!

A CAROL

Our Lord Who did the Ox command
    To kneel to Judah's King,
He binds His frost upon the land
    To ripen it for Spring—
To ripen it for Spring, good sirs,
    According to His Word;
Which well must be as ye can see—
    And who shall judge the Lord?

When we poor fenmen skate the ice
    Or shiver on the wold,
We hear the cry of a single tree
    That breaks her heart in the cold—
That breaks her heart in the cold, good sirs,
    And rendeth by the board;
Which well must be as ye can see—
    And who shall judge the Lord?

Her wood is crazed and little worth
    Excepting as to burn,
That we may warm and make our mirth
    Until the Spring return—
Until the Spring return, good sirs.
    When people walk abroad;

Which well must be as ye can see—
    And who shall judge the Lord?

God bless the master of this house.
    And all who sleep therein!
And guard the fens from pirate folk.
    And keep us all from sin,
To walk in honesty, good sirs,
    Of thought and deed and word!
Which shall befriend our latter end—
    And who shall judge the Lord?

'MY NEW-CUT ASHLAR'

My new-cut ashlar takes the light
Where crimson-blank the windows flare.
By my own work before the night,
Great Overseer, I make my prayer.

If there be good in that I wrought,
Thy Hand compelled it, Master, Thine—
Where I have failed to meet Thy Thought
I know, through Thee, the blame was mine.

One instant's toil to Thee denied
Stands all Eternity's offence.
Of that I did with Thee to guide
To Thee, through Thee, be excellence.

The depth and dream of my desire,
The bitter paths wherein I stray—
Thou knowest Who hath made the Fire,
Thou knowest Who hast made the Clay.

Who, lest all thought of Eden fade,
Bring'st Eden to the craftsman's brain—
Godlike to muse o'er his own Trade
And manlike stand with God again!

One stone the more swings into place
In that dread Temple of Thy worth.
It is enough that, through Thy Grace,
I saw nought common on Thy Earth.

Take not that vision from my ken—
Oh whatsoe'er may spoil or speed.
Help me to need no aid from men
That I may help such men as need!

EDDI'S SERVICE

(A.D. 687)

Eddi, priest of St. Wilfrid
    In the chapel at Manhood End,
Ordered a midnight service
    For such as cared to attend.

But the Saxons were keeping Christmas,
    And the night was stormy as well.
Nobody came to service
    Though Eddi rang the bell.

'Wicked weather for walking,'
    Said Eddi of Manhood End.
'But I must go on with the service
    For such as care to attend.'

The altar-candles were lighted,—
    An old marsh donkey came,
Bold as a guest invited,
    And stared at the guttering flame.

The storm beat on at the windows,
    The water splashed on the floor,

And a wet, yoke-weary bullock
    Pushed in through the open door.

'How do I know what is greatest,
    How do I know what is least?
That is My Father's business,'
    Said Eddi, Wilfrid's priest.

'But—three are gathered together—
    Listen to me and attend.
I bring good news, my brethren!'
    Said Eddi of Manhood End.

And he told the Ox of a Manger
    And a Stall in Bethlehem,
And he spoke to the Ass of a Rider,
    That rode to Jerusalem.

They steamed and dripped in the chancel,
    They listened and never stirred,
While, just as though they were Bishops,
    Eddi preached them The Word.

Till the gale blew off on the marshes
    And the windows showed the day,
And the Ox and the Ass together
    Wheeled and clattered away.

And when the Saxons mocked him,
    Said Eddi of Manhood End,
'I dare not shut His chapel
    On such as care to attend.'

SHIV AND THE GRASSHOPPER

Shiv, who poured the harvest and made the winds to blow,
Sitting at the doorways of a day of long ago,
Gave to each his portion, food and toil and fate,
From the King upon the *guddee* to the Beggar at the gate.
    All things made he—Shiva the Preserver.
    Mahadeo! Mahadeo! He made all,—
    Thorn for the camel, fodder for the kine,
    And mother's heart for sleepy head, O little son of mine!

Wheat he gave to rich folk, millet to the poor,
Broken scraps for holy men that beg from door to door;
Cattle to the tiger, carrion to the kite,
And rags and bones to wicked wolves without the wall at night.
Naught he found too lofty, none he saw too low—
Parbati beside him watched them come and go;
Thought to cheat her husband, turning Shiv to jest—
Stole the little grasshopper and hid it in her breast.
    So she tricked him, Shiva the Preserver.
    Mahadeo! Mahadeo! turn and see!
    Tall are the camels, heavy are the kine,
    But this was Least of Little Things, O little son of mine!

When the dole was ended, laughingly she said,
'Master, of a million mouths is not one unfed?'
Laughing, Shiv made answer, 'All have had their part,

Even he, the little one, hidden 'neath thy heart.'
From her breast she plucked it, Parbati the thief,
Saw the Least of Little Things gnawed a new-grown leaf!
Saw and feared and wondered, making prayer to Shiv,
Who hath surely given meat to all that live.

All things made he—Shiva the Preserver.
Mahadeo! Mahadeo! He made all,—
Thorn for the camel, fodder for the kine,
And mother's heart for sleepy head, O little son of mine!

THE FAIRIES' SIEGE

I have been given my charge to keep—
Well have I kept the same!
Playing with strife for the most of my life,
But this is a different game.
I'll not fight against swords unseen,
Or spears that I cannot view—
Hand him the keys of the place on your knees—
'Tis the Dreamer whose dreams come true!

Ask for his terms and accept them at once.
Quick, ere we anger him; go!
Never before have I flinched from the guns,
But this is a different show.
I'll not fight with the Herald of God
(I know what his Master can do!)
Open the gate, he must enter in state,
'Tis the Dreamer whose dreams come true!

I'd not give way for an Emperor,
I'd hold my road for a King—
To the Triple Crown I would not bow down—
But this is a different thing.
I'll not fight with the Powers of Air,
Sentry, pass him through!
Drawbridge let fall, it's the Lord of us all,
The Dreamer whose dreams come true!

A SONG TO MITHRAS

(Hymn of the 30th Legion: *circa* A.D. 350.)

Mithras, God of the Morning, our trumpets waken the Wall!
'Rome is above the Nations, but Thou art over all!'
Now as the names are answered and the guards are marched away,
Mithras, also a soldier, give us strength for the day!

Mithras, God of the Noontide, the heather swims in the heat.
Our helmets scorch our foreheads, our sandals burn our feet.
Now in the ungirt hour—now ere we blink and drowse,
Mithras, also a soldier, keep us true to our vows!

Mithras, God of the Sunset, low on the Western main—
Thou descending immortal, immortal to rise again!
Now when the watch is ended, now when the wine is drawn,
Mithras, also a soldier, keep us pure till the dawn!

Mithras, God of the Midnight, here where the great bull dies,
Look on thy children in darkness. Oh take our sacrifice!
Many roads thou hast fashioned—all of them lead to the Light:
Mithras, also a soldier, teach us to die aright!

THE NEW KNIGHTHOOD

Who gives him the Bath?
'I,' said the wet,
Rank Jungle-sweat,
'I'll give him the Bath!'

Who'll sing the psalms?
'We,' said the Palms.
'Ere the hot wind becalms,
We'll sing the psalms.'

Who lays on the sword?
'I,' said the Sun,
'Before he has done,
I'll lay on the sword.'

Who fastens his belt?
'I,' said Short-Rations,
'I know all the fashions
Of tightening a belt!'

Who gives him his spur?
'I,' said his Chief,
Exacting and brief,
'I'll give him the spur.'

Who'll shake his hand?
'I,' said the Fever,
'And I'm no deceiver,
I'll shake his hand.'

Who brings him the wine?
'I,' said Quinine,
'It's a habit of mine.
I'll come with the wine.'

Who'll put him to proof?
'I,' said All Earth,
'Whatever he's worth,
I'll put to the proof.'

Who'll choose him for Knight?
'I,' said his Mother,
'Before any other,
My very own Knight.'

And after this fashion, adventure to seek,
Was Sir Galahad made—as it might be last week!

OUTSONG IN THE JUNGLE

BALOO

FOR the sake of him who showed
One wise Frog the Jungle-Road,
Keep the Law the Man-Pack make
For thy blind old Baloo's sake!
Clean or tainted, hot or stale,
Hold it as it were the Trail,
Through the day and through the night,
Questing neither left nor right.
For the sake of him who loves
Thee beyond all else that moves,
When thy Pack would make thee pain,
Say: 'Tabaqui sings again.'
When thy Pack would work thee ill,
Say: 'Shere Khan is yet to kill.'
When the knife is drawn to slay,
Keep the Law and go thy way.
(Root and honey, palm and spathe,
Guard a cub from harm and scathe!)
Wood and Water, Wind and Tree,
Jungle-Favour go with thee!

KAA

Anger is the egg of Fear—
Only lidless eyes are clear.
Cobra-poison none may leech,
Even so with Cobra-speech.
Open talk shall call to thee
Strength, whose mate is Courtesy.
Send no lunge beyond thy length;
Lend no rotten bough thy strength.
Gauge thy gape with buck or goat,
Lest thine eye should choke thy throat
After gorging, wouldst thou sleep?
Look thy den be hid and deep,
Lest a wrong, by thee forgot,
Draw thy killer to the spot.
East and West and North and South,
Wash thy hide and close thy mouth.
(Pit and rift and blue pool-brim,
Middle-Jungle follow him!)
Wood and Water, Wind and Tree,
Jungle-Favour go with thee!

BAGHEERA

In the cage my life began;
Well I know the worth of Man.
By the Broken Lock that freed—
Man-cub, 'ware the Man-cub's breed!
Scenting-dew or starlight pale,
Choose no tangled tree-cat trail.
Pack or council, hunt or den,

Cry no truce with Jackal-Men.
Feed them silence when they say:
'Come with us an easy way.'
Feed them silence when they seek
Help of thine to hurt the weak.
Make no *bandar's* boast of skill;
Hold thy peace above the kill.
Let nor call nor song nor sign
Turn thee from thy hunting-line.
(Morning mist or twilight clear,
Serve him, Wardens of the Deer!)
Wood and Water, Wind and Tree,
Jungle-Favour go with thee!

THE THREE

On the trail that thou must tread
To the thresholds of our dread,
Where the Flower blossoms red;
Through the nights when thou shalt lie
Prisoned from our Mother-sky,
Hearing us, thy loves, go by;
In the dawns when thou shalt wake
To the toil thou canst not break,
Heartsick for the Jungle's sake:
Wood and Water, Wind and Tree,
Wisdom, Strength, and Courtesy,
Jungle-Favour go with thee!

HARP SONG OF THE DANE WOMEN

What is a woman that you forsake her,
And the hearth-fire and the home-acre,
To go with the old grey Widow-maker?

She has no house to lay a guest in—
But one chill bed for all to rest in,
That the pale suns and the stray bergs nest in.

She has no strong white arms to fold you,
But the ten-times-fingering weed to hold you—
Out on the rocks where the tide has rolled you.

Yet, when the signs of summer thicken,
And the ice breaks, and the birch-buds quicken,
Yearly you turn from our side, and sicken—

Sicken again for the shouts and the slaughters.
You steal away to the lapping waters,
And look at your ship in her winter quarters.

You forget our mirth, and talk at the tables,
The kine in the shed and the horse in the stables—
To pitch her sides and go over her cables.

Then you drive out where the storm-clouds swallow,
And the sound of your oar-blades, falling hollow.
Is all we have left through the months to follow.

Ah, what is Woman that you forsake her,
And the hearth-fire and the home-acre,
To go with the old grey Widow-maker?

THE THOUSANDTH MAN

One man in a thousand, Solomon says,
Will stick more close than a brother.
And it's worth while seeking him half your days
If you find him before the other.
Nine hundred and ninety-nine depend
On what the world sees in you,
But the Thousandth Man will stand your friend
With the whole round world agin you.

'Tis neither promise nor prayer nor show
Will settle the finding for 'ee.
Nine hundred and ninety-nine of 'em go
By your looks or your acts or your glory.
But if he finds you and you find him,
The rest of the world don't matter;
For the Thousandth Man will sink or swim
With you in any water.

You can use his purse with no more talk
Than he uses yours for his spendings,
And laugh and meet in your daily walk
As though there had been no lendings.
Nine hundred and ninety-nine of 'em call
For silver and gold in their dealings;

But the Thousandth Man he's worth 'em all.
Because you can show him your feelings.

His wrong's your wrong, and his right's your right,
In season or out of season.
Stand up and back it in all men's sight—
With *that* for your only reason!
Nine hundred and ninety-nine can't bide
The shame or mocking or laughter,
But the Thousandth Man will stand by your side
To the gallows-foot—and after!

THE WINNERS

What is the moral? Who rides may read.
When the night is thick and the tracks are blind
A friend at a pinch is a friend indeed,
But a fool to wait for the laggard behind.
Down to Gehenna or up to the Throne,
He travels the fastest who travels alone.

White hands cling to the tightened rein,
Slipping the spur from the booted heel,
Tenderest voices cry 'Turn again,'
Red lips tarnish the scabbarded steel,
High hopes faint on a warm hearth stone—
He travels the fastest who travels alone.

One may fall but he falls by himself—
Falls by himself with himself to blame,
One may attain and to him is pelf,
Loot of the city in Gold or Fame.
Plunder of earth shall be all his own
Who travels the fastest and travels alone.

Wherefore the more ye be holpen and stayed,
Stayed by a friend in the hour of toil,
Sing the heretical song I have made—
His be the labour and yours be the spoil,
Win by his aid and the aid disown—
He travels the fastest who travels alone!

A ST. HELENA LULLABY

'How far is St. Helena from a little child at play?'
What makes you want to wander there with all the world between?
Oh, Mother, call your son again or else he'll run away.
(No one thinks of winter when the grass is green!)

'How far is St. Helena from a fight in Paris street?'
I haven't time to answer now—the men are falling fast.
The guns begin to thunder, and the drums begin to beat.
(If you take the first step you will take the last!)

'How far is St. Helena from the field of Austerlitz?'
You couldn't hear me if I told—so loud the cannons roar.
But not so far for people who are living by their wits.
('Gay go up' means 'Gay go down' the wide world o'er!)

'How far is St. Helena from an Emperor of France?'
I cannot see—I cannot tell—the crowns they dazzle so.
The Kings sit down to dinner, and the Queens stand up to dance.
(After open weather you may look for snow!)

'How far is St. Helena from the Capes of Trafalgar?'
A longish way—a longish way—with ten year more to run.
It's South across the water underneath a setting star.
(What you cannot finish you must leave undone!)

'How far is St. Helena from the Beresina ice?'
An ill way—a chill way—the ice begins to crack.
But not so far for gentlemen who never took advice.
(When you can't go forward you must e'en come back!)

'How far is St. Helena from the field of Waterloo?'
A near way—a clear way—the ship will take you soon.
A pleasant place for gentlemen with little left to do,
(Morning never tries you till the afternoon!)

'How far from St. Helena to the Gate of Heaven's Grace?'
That no one knows—that no one knows—and no one ever will.
But fold your hands across your heart and cover up your face,
And after all your trapesings, child, lie still!

CHIL'S SONG

These were my companions going forth by night—
    (For Chil! Look you, for Chil!)
Now come I to whistle them the ending of the fight.
    (Chil! Vanguards of Chil!)
Word they gave me overhead of quarry newly slain,
Word I gave them underfoot of buck upon the plain.
Here's an end of every trail—they shall not speak again!

They that called the hunting-cry—they that followed fast—
    (For Chil! Look you, for Chil!)
They that bade the sambhur wheel, or pinned him as he passed—
    (Chil! Vanguards of Chil!)
They that lagged behind the scent—they that ran before,
They that shunned the level horn—they that overbore,
Here's an end of every trail—they shall not follow more.

These were my companions. Pity 'twas they died!
    (For Chil! Look you, for Chil!)
Now come I to comfort them that knew them in their pride.
    (Chil! Vanguards of Chil!)
Tattered flank and sunken eye, open mouth and red,
Locked and lank and lone they lie, the dead upon their dead.
Here's an end of every trail—and here my hosts are fed!

THE CAPTIVE

Not with an outcry to Allah nor any complaining
He answered his name at the muster and stood to the chaining.
When the twin anklets were nipped on the leg-bars that held them,
He brotherly greeted the armourers stooping to weld them.
Ere the sad dust of the marshalled feet of the chain-gang swallowed
    him,
Observing him nobly at ease, I alighted and followed him.
Thus we had speech by the way, but not touching his sorrow—
Rather his red Yesterday and his regal Tomorrow,
Wherein he statelily moved to the clink of his chains unregarded,
Nowise abashed but contented to drink of the potion awarded.
Saluting aloofly his Fate, he made swift with his story,
And the words of his mouth were as slaves spreading carpets of glory
Embroidered with names of the Djinns—a miraculous weaving—
But the cool and perspicuous eye overbore unbelieving.
So I submitted myself to the limits of rapture—
Bound by this man we had bound, amid captives his capture—
Till he returned me to earth and the visions departed.
But on him be the Peace and the Blessing; for he was great-hearted!

THE PUZZLER

The Celt in all his variants from Builth to Ballyhoo,
His mental processes are plain—one knows what he will do,
And can logically predicate his finish by his start;
But the English—ah, the English—they are quite a race apart.

Their psychology is bovine, their outlook crude and raw.
They abandon vital matters to be tickled with a straw,
But the straw that they were tickled with—the chaff that they were fed
    with—
They convert into a weaver's beam to break their foeman's head with.

For undemocratic reasons and for motives not of State,
They arrive at their conclusions—largely inarticulate.
Being void of self-expression they confide their views to none;
But sometimes in a smoking-room, one learns why things were done.

Yes, sometimes in a smoking-room, through clouds of 'Ers' and 'Ums,'
Obliquely and by inference illumination comes,
On some step that they have taken, or some action they approve—
Embellished with the *argot* of the Upper Fourth Remove.

In telegraphic sentences, half nodded to their friends,
They hint a matter's inwardness—and there the matter ends.
And while the Celt is talking from Valencia to Kirkwall,
The English—ah, the English!—don't say anything at all!

HADRAMAUTI

Who knows the heart of the Christian? How does he reason?
What are his measures and balances? Which is his season
For laughter, forbearance or bloodshed, and what devils move him
When he arises to smite us? *I* do not love him.

He invites the derision of strangers—he enters all places.
Booted, bareheaded he enters. With shouts and embraces
He asks of us news of the household whom we reckon nameless.
Certainly Allah created him forty-fold shameless.

So it is not in the Desert. One came to me weeping—
The Avenger of Blood on his track—I took him in keeping.
Demanding not whom he had slain, I refreshed him, I fed him
As he were even a brother. But Eblis had bred him.

He was the son of an ape, ill at ease in his clothing,
He talked with his head, hands and feet. I endured him with loathing.
Whatever his spirit conceived his countenance showed it
As a frog shows in a mud-puddle. Yet I abode it!

I fingered my beard and was dumb, in silence confronting him.
His soul was too shallow for silence, e'en with Death hunting him.
I said: 'Tis his weariness speaks,' but, when he had rested,
He chirped in my face like some sparrow, and, presently, jested!

Wherefore slew I that stranger? He brought me dishonour.
I saddled my mare, Bijli, I set him upon her.
I gave him rice and goat's flesh. He bared me to laughter.
When he was gone from my tent, swift I followed after,
Taking my sword in my hand. The hot wine had filled him.
Under the stars he mocked me—therefore I killed him!

CHAPTER HEADINGS

THE NAULAHKA

We meet in an evil land
That is near to the gates of hell.
I wait for thy command
To serve, to speed or withstand.
And thou sayest, I do not well?

Oh Love, the flowers so red
Are only tongues of flame,
The earth is full of the dead,
The new-killed, restless dead.
There is danger beneath and o'erhead,
And I guard thy gates in fear
    Of peril and jeopardy,
Of words thou canst not hear,
Of signs thou canst not see—
And thou sayest 'tis ill that I came?

This I saw when the rites were done,
And the lamps were dead and the Gods alone,
And the grey snake coiled on the altar stone—
Ere I fled from a Fear that I could not see,
And the Gods of the East made mouths at me.

* * * * *

Now it is not good for the Christian's health to hustle the Aryan brown,
For the Christian riles, and the Aryan smiles and he weareth the Christian
    down;
And the end of the fight is a tombstone white with the name of the late
    deceased,
And the epitaph drear: 'A fool lies here who tried to hustle the East.'

* * * * *

Beat off in our last fight were we?
The greater need to seek the sea.
For Fortune changeth as the moon
To caravel and picaroon.
Then Eastward Ho! or Westward Ho!
Whichever wind may meetest blow.
Our quarry sails on either sea,
Fat prey for such bold lads as we.
And every sun-dried buccaneer
Must hand and reef and watch and steer.
And bear great wrath of sea and sky
Before the plate-ships wallow by.
Now, as our tall bows take the foam,
Let no man turn his heart to home,
Save to desire treasure more,
And larger warehouse for his store,
When treasure won from Santos Bay
Shall make our sea-washed village gay.

* * * * *

Because I sought it far from men,
In deserts and alone,

I found it burning overhead,
The jewel of a Throne.

Because I sought—I sought it so
And spent my days to find—
It blazed one moment ere it left
The blacker night behind.

        *   *   *   *   *

When a lover hies abroad.
Looking for his love,
Azrael smiling sheathes his sword,
Heaven smiles above.
Earth and sea
His servants be,
And to lesser compass round,
That his love be sooner found.

        *   *   *   *   *

There was a strife 'twixt man and maid—
Oh that was at the birth of time!
But what befell 'twixt man and maid,
Oh that's beyond the grip of rhyme.
'Twas, 'Sweet, I must not bide with you,'
And 'Love, I cannot bide alone';
For both were young and both were true,
And both were hard as the nether stone.

        *   *   *   *   *

There is pleasure in the wet, wet clay,
When the artist's hand is potting it;
There is pleasure in the wet, wet lay,
When the poet's pad is blotting it;
There is pleasure in the shine of your picture on the line
At the Royal Acade-my;
But the pleasure felt in these is as chalk to Cheddar cheese
When it comes to a well-made Lie:
To a quite unwreckable Lie,
To a most impeccable Lie!
To a water-tight, fire-proof, angle-iron, sunk-hinge, time-lock, steel-face
    Lie!
Not a private hansom Lie,
But a pair-and-brougham Lie,
Not a little-place-at-Tooting, but a country-house-with-shooting
And a ring-fence-deer-park Lie.

∗ ∗ ∗ ∗ ∗

  We be the Gods of the East—
      Older than all—
  Masters of Mourning and Feast
      How shall we fall?

  Will they gape for the husks that ye proffer
      Or yearn to your song?
  And we—have we nothing to offer
      Who ruled them so long—
In the fume of the incense, the clash of the cymbal, the blare of the
    conch and the gong?

Over the strife of the schools
    Low the day burns—
Back with the kine from the pools
    Each one returns
To the life that he knows where the altar-flame glows and the *tulsi* is
trimmed in the urns.

THE LIGHT THAT FAILED

So we settled it all when the storm was done
As comfy as comfy could be;
And I was to wait in the barn, my dears,
Because I was only three,
And Teddy would run to the rainbow's foot
Because he was five and a man;
And that's how it all began, my dears,
And that's how it all began.

* * * * *

'If I have taken the common clay
    And wrought it cunningly
In the shape of a God that was digged a clod,
    The greater honour to me.'
'If thou hast taken the common clay,
    And thy hands be not free
From the taint of the soil, thou hast made thy spoil
    The greater shame to thee.'

* * * * *

The wolf-cub at even lay hid in the corn,
Where the smoke of the cooking hung grey:
He knew where the doe made a couch for her fawn,

And he looked to his strength for his prey.
But the moon swept the smoke-wreaths away,
And he turned from his meal in the villager's close,
And he bayed to the moon as she rose.

* * * * *

The lark will make her hymn to God,
The partridge call her brood,
While I forget the heath I trod,
The fields wherein I stood.

Tis dule to know not night from morn,
But greater dule to know
I can but hear the hunter's horn
That once I used to blow.

* * * * *

There were three friends that buried the fourth,
The mould in his mouth and the dust in his eyes,
And they went south and east and north—
The strong man fights but the sick man dies.

There were three friends that spoke of the dead—
The strong man fights but the sick man dies—
'And would he were here with us now,' they said,
'The sun in our face and the wind in our eyes.'

* * * * *

Yet at the last, ere our spearmen had found him,
Yet at the last, ere a sword-thrust could save,

Yet at the last, with his masters around him,
He spoke of the Faith as a master to slave.
Yet at the last, though the Kafirs had maimed him,
Broken by bondage and wrecked by the reiver,
Yet at the last, tho' the darkness had claimed him,
He called upon Allah, and died a Believer!

GALLIO'S SONG

(And Gallio cared for none of these things.—ACTS xviii. 17)

All day long to the judgment-seat
The crazed Provincials drew—
All day long at their ruler's feet
Howled for the blood of the Jew.
Insurrection with one accord
Banded itself and woke,
And Paul was about to open his mouth
When Achaia's Deputy spoke—

'Whether the God descend from above
Or the Man ascend upon high,
Whether this maker of tents be Jove
Or a younger deity—
I will be no judge between your gods
And your godless bickerings.
Lictor, drive them hence with rods—
I care for none of these things!

'Were it a question of lawful due
Or Cæsar's rule denied,
Reason would I should bear with you
And order it well to be tried;
But this is a question of words and names.

I know the strife it brings.
I will not pass upon any your claims.
I care for none of these things.

'One thing only I see most clear,
As I pray you also see.
Claudius Cæsar hath set me here
Rome's Deputy to be.
It is Her peace that ye go to break—
Not mine, nor any king's.
But, touching your clamour of "Conscience sake,"
I care for none of these things.

'Whether ye rise for the sake of a creed,
Or riot in hope of spoil,
Equally will I punish the deed,
Equally check the broil;
Nowise permitting injustice at all
From whatever doctrine it springs—
But—whether ye follow Priapus or Paul,
I care for none of these things.'

THE BEES AND THE FLIES

A farmer of the Augustan Age
Perused in Virgil's golden page,
The story of the secret won
From Proteus by Cyrene's son—
How the dank sea-god showed the swain
Means to restore his hives again.
More briefly, how a slaughtered bull
Breeds honey by the bellyful.

The egregious rustic put to death
A bull by stopping of its breath,
Disposed the carcass in a shed
With fragrant herbs and branches spread,
And, having thus performed the charm,
Sat down to wait the promised swarm.

Nor waited long. The God of Day
Impartial, quickening with his ray
Evil and good alike, beheld
The carcass—and the carcass swelled.
Big with new birth the belly heaves
Beneath its screen of scented leaves.
Past any doubt, the bull conceives!

The farmer bids men bring more hives
To house the profit that arrives;
Prepares on pan, and key and kettle,
Sweet music that shall make 'em settle;
But when to crown the work he goes,
Gods! what a stink salutes his nose!

Where are the honest toilers? Where
The gravid mistress of their care?
A busy scene, indeed, he sees,
But not a sign or sound of bees.
Worms of the riper grave unhid
By any kindly coffin lid,
Obscene and shameless to the light,
Seethe in insatiate appetite,
Through putrid offal, while above
The hissing blow-fly seeks his love,
Whose offspring, supping where they supt,
Consume corruption twice corrupt.

ROAD-SONG OF THE *BANDAR-LOG*

Here we go in a flung festoon,
Half-way up to the jealous moon!
Don't you envy our pranceful bands?
Don't you wish you had extra hands?
Wouldn't you like if your tails were—*so*—
Curved in the shape of a Cupid's bow?
    Now you're angry, but—never mind,
    Brother, thy tail hangs down behind!

Here we sit in a branchy row,
Thinking of beautiful things we know;
Dreaming of deeds that we mean to do,
All complete, in a minute or two—
Something noble and grand and good,
Won by merely wishing we could.
    Now we're going to—never mind,
    Brother, thy tail hangs down behind!

All the talk we ever have heard
Uttered by bat or beast or bird—
Hide or fin or scale or feather—
Jabber it quickly and all together!
Excellent! Wonderful! Once again!

Now we are talking just like men.
>   Let's pretend we are . . . never mind,
>   *Brother, thy tail hangs down behind!*
>   This is the way of the Monkey-kind!

Then join our leaping lines that scumfish through the pines,
That rocket by where, light and high, the wild-grape swings.
By the rubbish in our wake, and the noble noise we make,
Be sure, be sure, we're going to do some splendid things.

'OUR FATHERS ALSO'

Thrones, Powers, Dominions, Peoples, Kings,
Are changing 'neath our hand;
Our fathers also see these things
But they do not understand.

By—they are by with mirth and tears,
Wit or the works of Desire—
Cushioned about on the kindly years
Between the wall and the fire.

The grapes are pressed, the corn is shocked—
Standeth no more to glean;
For the Gates of Love and Learning locked
When they went out between.

All lore our Lady Venus bares,
Signalled it was or told
By the dear lips long given to theirs
And longer to the mould.

All Profit, all Device, all Truth
Written it was or said
By the mighty men of their mighty youth,
Which is mighty being dead.

The film that floats before their eyes
The Temple's Veil they call;
And the dust that on the Shewbread lies
Is holy over all.

Warn them of seas that slip our yoke
Of slow-conspiring stars—
The ancient Front of Things unbroke
But heavy with new wars?

By—they are by with mirth and tears,
Wit or the waste of Desire—
Cushioned about on the kindly years
Between the wall and the fire.

A BRITISH-ROMAN SONG

(A.D. 406)

My father's father saw it not,
    And I, belike, shall never come,
To look on that so-holy spot—
      The very Rome—

Crowned by all Time, all Art, all Might,
    The equal work of Gods and Man,
City beneath whose oldest height—
      The Race began!

Soon to send forth again a brood,
    Unshakeable, we pray, that clings,
To Rome's thrice-hammered hardihood—
      In arduous things.

Strong heart with triple armour bound,
    Beat strongly, for thy life-blood runs,
Age after Age, the Empire round—
      In us thy Sons.

Who, distant from the Seven Hills,
    Loving and serving much, require
Thee—*thee* to guard 'gainst home-born ills,
      The Imperial Fire!

A PICT SONG

Rome never looks where she treads.
    Always her heavy hooves fall,
On our stomachs, our hearts or our heads;
    And Rome never heeds when we bawl.
Her sentries pass on—that is all,
    And we gather behind them in hordes,
And plot to reconquer the Wall,
    With only our tongues for our swords.

We are the Little Folk—we!
    Too little to love or to hate.
Leave us alone and you'll see
    How we can drag down the State!
We are the worm in the wood!
    We are the rot at the root!
We are the germ in the blood!
    We are the thorn in the foot!

Mistletoe killing an oak—
    Rats gnawing cables in two—
Moths making holes in a cloak—
    How they must love what they do!
Yes—and we Little Folk too,
    We are busy as they—

Working our works out of view—
    Watch, and you'll see it some day!

No indeed! We are not strong,
    But we know Peoples that are.
Yes, and we'll guide them along,
    To smash and destroy you in War!
We shall be slaves just the same?
    Yes, we have always been slaves,
But you—you will die of the shame,
    And then we shall dance on your graves!

We are the Little Folk, we, etc.

THE STRANGER

The Stranger within my gate,
    He may be true or kind.
But he does not talk my talk—
    I cannot feel his mind.
I see the face and the eyes and the mouth,
    But not the soul behind.

The men of my own stock
    They may do ill or well,
But they tell the lies I am wonted to,
    They are used to the lies I tell.
We do not need interpreters
    When we go to buy and sell.

The Stranger within my gates,
    He may be evil or good,
But I cannot tell what powers control—
    What reasons sway his mood;
Nor when the Gods of his far-off land
    May repossess his blood.

The men of my own stock,
    Bitter bad they may be,
But, at least, they hear the things I hear,
    And see the things I see;

And whatever I think of them and their likes
    They think of the likes of me.

This was my father's belief
    And this is also mine:
Let the corn be all one sheaf—
    And the grapes be all one vine,
Ere our children's teeth are set on edge
    By bitter bread and wine.

'RIMINI'

(Marching Song of a Roman Legion of the Later Empire)

When I left home for Lalage's sake
By the Legions' road to Rimini,
She vowed her heart was mine to take
With me and my shield to Rimini—
(Till the Eagles flew from Rimini!)
And I've tramped Britain, and I've tramped Gaul,
And the Pontic shore where the snow-flakes fall
As white as the neck of Lalage—
(As cold as the heart of Lalage!)
And I've lost Britain, and I've lost Gaul,
And I've lost Rome, and worst of all,
I've lost Lalage!

When you go by the Via Aurelia,
As thousands have travelled before,
Remember the Luck of the Soldier
Who never saw Rome any more!
Oh dear was the sweetheart that kissed him
And dear was the mother that bore,
But his shield was picked up in the heather,
And he never saw Rome any more!

And *he* left Rome, etc.

94

When you go by the Via Aurelia
That runs from the City to Gaul,
Remember the Luck of the Soldier
Who rose to be master of all!
He carried the sword and the buckler,
He mounted his guard on the Wall,
Till the Legions elected him Cæsar,
And he rose to be master of all!

And *he* left Rome, etc.

It's twenty-five marches to Narbo,
It's forty-five more up the Rhone,
And the end may be death in the heather
Or life on an Emperor's throne.

But whether the Eagles obey us,
Or we go to the Ravens—alone,
I'd sooner be Lalage's lover
Than sit on an Emperor's throne!

We've *all* left Rome for Lalage's sake, etc.

'POOR HONEST MEN'

(A.D. 1800)

Your jar of Virginny
Will cost you a guinea
Which you reckon too much by five shillings or ten;
But light your churchwarden
And judge it according,
When I've told you the troubles of poor honest men!

From the Capes of the Delaware,
As you are well aware,
We sail with tobacco for England—but then,
Our own British cruisers,
They watch us come through, sirs,
And they press half a score of us poor honest men!

Or if by quick sailing
(Thick weather prevailing)
We leave them behind (as we do now and then)
We are sure of a gun from
Each frigate we run from,
Which is often destruction to poor honest men!

Broadsides the Atlantic
We tumble short-handed,

With shot-holes to plug and new canvas to bend,
And off the Azores,
Dutch, Dons and Monsieurs
Are waiting to terrify poor honest men.

Napoleon's embargo
Is laid on all cargo
Which comfort or aid to King George may intend;
And since roll, twist and leaf,
Of all comforts is chief,
They try for to steal it from poor honest men!

With no heart for fight,
We take refuge in flight
But fire as we run, our retreat to defend,
Until our stern-chasers
Cut up her fore-braces,
And she flies up the wind from us poor honest men!

Twix' the Forties and Fifties,
South-eastward the drift is,
And so, when we think we are making Land's End,
Alas! it is Ushant
With half the King's Navy,
Blockading French ports against poor honest men!

But they may not quit station
(Which is our salvation),
So swiftly we stand to the Nor'ard again;
And finding the tail of
A homeward-bound convoy,
We slip past the Scillies like poor honest men.

Twix' the Lizard and Dover,
We hand our stuff over,
Though I may not inform how we do it, nor when.
But a light on each quarter
Low down on the water
Is well understanded by poor honest men!

Even then we have dangers,
From meddlesome strangers,
Who spy on our business and are not content
To take a smooth answer,
Except with a handspike . . .
And they say they are murdered by poor honest men!

To be drowned or be shot
Is our natural lot,
Why should we, moreover, be hanged in the end—
After all our great pains
For to dangle in chains
As though we were smugglers, not poor honest men?

'WHEN THE GREAT ARK'

When the Great Ark, in Vigo Bay,
    Rode stately through the half-manned fleet,
From every ship about her way
    She heard the mariners entreat—
'Before we take the seas again,
Let down your boats and send us men!

'We have no lack of victual here
    With work—God knows!—enough for all,
To hand and reef and watch and steer,
    Because our present strength is small.
While your three decks are crowded so
Your crews can scarcely stand or go.

'In war, your numbers do but raise
    Confusion and divided will;
In storm, the mindless deep obeys
    Not multitudes but single skill;
In calm, your numbers, closely pressed.
Do breed a mutiny or pest.

'We, even on unchallenged seas,
    Dare not adventure where we would,
But forfeit brave advantages
    For lack of men to make 'em good;
Whereby, to England's double cost.
Honour and profit both are lost!'

PROPHETS AT HOME

Prophets have honour all over the Earth,
    Except in the village where they were born.
Where such as knew them boys from birth,
    Nature-ally hold 'em in scorn.

When Prophets are naughty and young and vain,
    They make a won'erful grievance of it;
(You can see by their writings how they complain),
    But O, 'tis won'erful good for the Prophet!

There's nothing Nineveh Town can give
    (Nor being swallowed by whales between),
Makes up for the place where a man's folk live,
    Which don't care nothing what he has been.
He might ha' been that, or he might ha' been this,
    But they love and they hate him for what he is.

JUBAL AND TUBAL CAIN

Jubal sang of the Wrath of God
    And the curse of thistle and thorn—
But Tubal got him a pointed rod,
    And scrabbled the earth for corn.
    Old—old as that early mould,
        Young as the sprouting grain—
    Yearly green is the strife between
        Jubal and Tubal Cain!

Jubal sang of the new-found sea,
    And the love that its waves divide—
But Tubal hollowed a fallen tree
    And passed to the further side.
    Black—black as the hurricane-wrack,
        Salt as the under-main—
    Bitter and cold is the hate they hold—
        Jubal and Tubal Cain!

Jubal sang of the golden years
    When wars and wounds shall cease—
But Tubal fashioned the hand-flung spears
    And showèd his neighbours peace.
    New—new as the Nine point Two,
        Older than Lamech's slain—

Roaring and loud is the feud avowed
    Twix' Jubal and Tubal Cain!

Jubal sang of the cliffs that bar
    And the peaks that none may crown—
But Tubal clambered by jut and scar
    And there he builded a town.
    High—high as the snowsheds lie,
        Low as the culverts drain—
    Wherever they be they can never agree—
        Jubal and Tubal Cain!

THE VOORTREKKER

The gull shall whistle in his wake, the blind wave break in fire.
He shall fulfil God's utmost will, unknowing his desire.
And he shall see old planets change and alien stars arise,
And give the gale his seaworn sail in shadow of new skies.
Strong lust of gear shall drive him forth and hunger arm his hand,
To win his food from the desert rude, his pittance from the sand.
His neighbours' smoke shall vex his eyes, their voices break his rest,
He shall go forth till south is north sullen and dispossessed.
He shall desire loneliness and his desire shall bring,
Hard on his heels, a thousand wheels, a People and a King.
He shall come back on his own track, and by his scarce-cooled camp
There shall he meet the roaring street, the derrick and the stamp:
There he shall blaze a nation's ways with hatchet and with brand,
Till on his last-won wilderness an Empire's outposts stand.

A SCHOOL SONG

'Let us now praise famous men'—
  Men of little showing—
For their work continueth,
And their work continueth,
Broad and deep continueth,
  Greater than their knowing!

Western wind and open surge
  Took us from our mothers.
Flung us on a naked shore
(Twelve bleak houses by the shore!
Seven summers by the shore!)
  'Mid two hundred brothers.

There we met with famous men
  Set in office o'er us;
And they beat on us with rods—
Faithfully with many rods—
Daily beat on us with rods,
  For the love they bore us!

Out of Egypt unto Troy—
  Over Himalaya—
Far and sure our bands have gone—
Hy-Brasil or Babylon,

Islands of the Southern Run,
    And Cities of Cathaia!

And we all praise famous men—
    Ancients of the College;
For they taught us common sense—
Tried to teach us common sense—
Truth and God's Own Common Sense,
    Which is more than knowledge!

Each degree of Latitude
    Strung about Creation
Seeth one or more of us
(Of one muster each of us),
Diligent in that he does,
    Keen in his vocation.

This we learned from famous men,
    Knowing not its uses,
When they showed, in daily work,
Man must finish off his work—
Right or wrong, his daily work—
    And without excuses.

Servants of the Staff and chain,
    Mine and fuse and grapnel—
Some before the face of Kings,
Stand before the face of Kings;
Bearing gifts to divers Kings—
    Gifts of case and shrapnel.

This we learned from famous men
　　Teaching in our borders,
Who declarèd it was best,
Safest, easiest, and best—
Expeditious, wise, and best—
　　To obey your orders.

Some beneath the further stars
　　Bear the greater burden:
Set to serve the lands they rule,
(Save he serve no man may rule),
Serve and love the lands they rule;
　　Seeking praise nor guerdon.

This we learned from famous men,
　　Knowing not we learned it.
Only, as the years went by—
Lonely, as the years went by—
Far from help as years went by,
　　Plainer we discerned it.

Wherefore praise we famous men
　　From whose bays we borrow—
They that put aside Today—
All the joys of their Today—
And with toil of their Today
　　Bought for us Tomorrow!

Bless and praise we famous men—
Men of little showing—
For their work continueth,
And their work continueth,
Broad and deep continueth,
Great beyond their knowing!

THE LAW OF THE JUNGLE

Now this is the Law of the Jungle—as old and as true as the sky;
And the Wolf that shall keep it may prosper, but the Wolf that shall break it must die.

As the creeper that girdles the tree-trunk the Law runneth forward and back—
For the strength of the Pack is the Wolf, and the strength of the Wolf is the Pack.

Wash daily from nose-tip to tail-tip; drink deeply, but never too deep;
And remember the night is for hunting, and forget not the day is for sleep.

The Jackal may follow the Tiger, but, Cub, when thy whiskers are grown,
Remember the Wolf is a hunter—go forth and get food of thine own.

Keep peace with the Lords of the Jungle—the Tiger, the Panther, the Bear;
And trouble not Hathi the Silent, and mock not the Boar in his lair.

When Pack meets with Pack in the Jungle, and neither will go from the trail,
Lie down till the leaders have spoken—it may be fair words shall prevail.

When ye fight with a Wolf of the Pack, ye must fight him alone and afar,
Lest others take part in the quarrel, and the Pack be diminished by war.

The Lair of the Wolf is his refuge, and where he has made him his home,
Not even the Head Wolf may enter, not even the Council may come.

The Lair of the Wolf is his refuge, but where he has digged it too plain,
The Council shall send him a message, and so he shall change it again.

If ye kill before midnight, be silent, and wake not the woods with your bay,
Lest ye frighten the deer from the crops, and the brothers go empty away.

Ye may kill for yourselves, and your mates, and your cubs as they need, and ye can;
But kill not for pleasure of killing, and *seven times never kill Man!*

If ye plunder his Kill from a weaker, devour not all in thy pride;
Pack-Right is the right of the meanest; so leave him the head and the hide.

The Kill of the Pack is the meat of the Pack. Ye must eat where it lies;
And no one may carry away of that meat to his lair, or he dies.

The Kill of the Wolf is the meat of the Wolf. He may do what he will,
But, till he has given permission, the Pack may not eat of that Kill.

Cub-Right is the right of the Yearling. From all of his Pack he may claim
Full-gorge when the killer has eaten; and none may refuse him the same.

Lair-Right is the right of the Mother. From all of her year she may claim
One haunch of each kill for her litter; and none may deny her the same.

Cave-Right is the right of the Father—to hunt by himself for his own:
He is freed of all calls to the Pack; he is judged by the Council alone.

Because of his age and his cunning, because of his gripe and his paw,
In all that the Law leaveth open, the word of the Head Wolf is Law.

Now these are the Laws of the Jungle, and many and mighty are they;
But the head and the hoof of the Law and the haunch and the hump is—Obey!

'A SERVANT WHEN HE REIGNETH'

(For three things the earth is disquieted, and for four which it cannot bear: for a servant when he reigneth; and a fool when he is filled with meat; for an odious woman when she is married; and an handmaid that is heir to her mistress.—PROV. XXX. 21, 22, 23.)

Three things make earth unquiet,
And four she cannot brook;
The godly Agur counted them
And put them in a book—
Those Four Tremendous Curses
With which mankind is cursed:
But a Servant when He Reigneth
Old Agur counted first.

An Handmaid that is Mistress
We need not call upon,
A Fool when he is full of Meat
Will fall asleep anon.
An Odious Woman Married
May bear a babe and mend.
But a Servant when He Reigneth
Is Confusion to the end.

His feet are swift to tumult,
His hands are slow to toil,

His ears are deaf to reason,
His lips are loud in broil.
He knows no use for power
Except to show his might,
He gives no heed to judgment
Unless it prove him right.

Because he served a master
Before his Kingship came,
And hid in all disaster
Behind his master's name,
So, when his Folly opens
The unnecessary hells,
A Servant when He Reigneth
Throws the blame on some one else.

His vows are lightly spoken,
His faith is hard to bind.
His trust is easy broken,
He fears his fellow-kind.
The nearest mob will move him
To break the pledge he gave—
Oh a Servant when He Reigneth
Is more than ever slave!

'OUR FATHERS OF OLD'

Excellent herbs had our fathers of old—
    Excellent herbs to ease their pain—
Alexanders and Marigold,
    Eyebright, Orris, and Elecampane.
Basil, Rocket, Valerian, Rue,
    (Almost singing themselves they run)
Vervain, Dittany, Call-me-to-you—
    Cowslip, Melilot, Rose of the Sun.
        Anything green that grew out of the mould
        Was an excellent herb to our fathers of old.

Wonderful tales had our fathers of old—
    Wonderful tales of the herbs and the stars—
The Sun was Lord of the Marigold,
    Basil and Rocket belonged to Mars.
Pat as a sum in division it goes—
    (Every plant had a star bespoke)—
Who but Venus should govern the Rose?
    Who but Jupiter own the Oak?
        Simply and gravely the facts are told
        In the wonderful books of our fathers of old.

Wonderful little, when all is said,
    Wonderful little our fathers knew.
Half their remedies cured you dead—

Most of their teaching was quite untrue—
'Look at the stars when a patient is ill,
     (Dirt has nothing to do with disease,)
Bleed and blister as much as you will,
     Blister and bleed him as oft as you please.'
          Whence enormous and manifold
          Errors were made by our fathers of old.

Yet when the sickness was sore in the land,
     And neither planets nor herbs assuaged,
They took their lives in their lancet-hand
     And, oh, what a wonderful war they waged!
Yes, when the crosses were chalked on the door—
     (Yes, when the terrible dead-cart rolled,)
Excellent courage our fathers bore—
     Excellent heart had our fathers of old.
          None too learned, but nobly bold
          Into the fight went our fathers of old.

If it be certain, as Galen says,
     And sage Hippocrates holds as much—
'That those afflicted by doubts and dismays
     Are mightily helped by a dead man's touch',
Then, be good to us, stars above!
     Then, be good to us, herbs below!
We are afflicted by what we can prove,
     We are distracted by what we know—
          So—ah, so!
          Down from your heaven or up from your mould,
          Send us the hearts of our fathers of old!

THE HERITAGE

Our Fathers in a wondrous age,
    Ere yet the earth was small,
Ensured to us an heritage,
    And doubted not at all
That we, the children of their heart,
    Which then did beat so high,
In later time should play like part
    For our posterity.

A thousand years they steadfast built,
    To 'vantage us and ours,
The Walls that were a world's despair,
    The sea-constraining Towers:
Yet in their midmost pride they knew,
    And unto Kings made known,
Not all from these their strength they drew,
    Their faith from brass or stone.

Youth's passion, manhood's fierce intent.
    With age's judgment wise,
They spent, and counted not they spent.
    At daily sacrifice.
Not lambs alone nor purchased doves
    Or tithe of trader's gold—

Their lives most dear, their dearer loves,
 They offered up of old.

Refraining e'en from lawful things.
 They bowed the neck to bear
The unadornèd yoke that brings
 Stark toil and sternest care.
Wherefore through them is Freedom sure;
 Wherefore through them we stand
From all but sloth and pride secure,
 In a delightsome land.

Then, fretful, murmur not they gave
 So great a charge to keep.
Nor dream that awestruck Time shall save
 Their labour while we sleep.
Dear-bought and clear, a thousand year,
 Our fathers' title runs.
Make we likewise their sacrifice,
 Defrauding not our sons.

CHAPTER HEADINGS

'BEAST AND MAN IN INDIA'

They killed a child to please the Gods
In earth's young penitence,
And I have bled in that Babe's stead
Because of innocence.

I bear the sins of sinful men
That have no sin of my own,
They drive me forth to Heaven's wrath
Unpastured and alone.

I am the meat of sacrifice,
The ransom of man's guilt,
For they give my life to the altar-knife
Wherever shrine is built.

> *The Goat.*

Between the waving tufts of jungle-grass,
Up from the river as the twilight falls,
Across the dust-beclouded plain they pass
On to the village walls.

Great is the sword and mighty is the pen,
But greater far the labouring ploughman's blade,
For on its oxen and its husbandmen
An Empire's strength is laid.

The Oxen.

The torn boughs trailing o'er the tusks aslant,
The saplings reeling in the path he trod,
Declare his might—our lord the Elephant,
Chief of the ways of God.

The black bulk heaving where the oxen pant,
The bowed head toiling where the guns careen,
Declare our might—our slave the Elephant
And servant of the Queen.

The Elephant.

Dark children of the mere and marsh,
Wallow and waste and lea,
Outcaste they wait at the village gate
With folk of low degree.

Their pasture is in no man's land.
Their food the cattle's scorn,
Their rest is mire and their desire
The thicket and the thorn.

But woe to those who break their sleep,
And woe to those who dare
To rouse the herd-bull from his keep,
The wild boar from his lair!

Pigs and Buffaloes.

The beasts are very wise,
Their mouths are clean of lies,
They talk one to the other,
Bullock to bullock's brother
Resting after their labours,
Each in stall with his neighbours.
But man with goad and whip,
Breaks up their fellowship,
Shouts in their silky ears
Filling their souls with fears.
When he has ploughed the land,
He says: 'They understand.'
But the beasts in stall together,
Freed from the yoke and tether,
Say as the torn flanks smoke:
'Nay, 'twas the whip that spoke.'

LIFE'S HANDICAP

The doors were wide, the story saith,
Out of the night came the patient wraith.
He might not speak, and he could not stir
A hair of the Baron's minniver.
Speechless and strengthless, a shadow thin,
He roved the castle to find his kin.
And oh! 'twas a piteous sight to see
The dumb ghost follow his enemy!

The Return of Imray.

Before my spring I garnered autumn's gain,
Out of her time my field was white with grain,
The year gave up her secrets, to my woe.
Forced and deflowered each sick season lay
In mystery of increase and decay;
I saw the sunset ere men see the day,
Who am too wise in all I should not know.

Without Benefit of Clergy.

KIM

Unto whose use the pregnant suns are poised,
With idiot moons and stars retracting stars?
Creep thou between—thy coming's all unnoised.
Heaven hath her high, as Earth her baser, wars.
Heir to these tumults, this affright, that fray
(By Adam's, fathers', own, sin bound alway);
Peer up, draw out thy horoscope and say
Which planet mends thy threadbare fate, or mars.

MANY INVENTIONS

And if ye doubt the tale I tell,
Steer through the South Pacific swell;
Go where the branching coral hives
Unending strife of endless lives,
Where, leagued about the 'wildered boat,
The rainbow jellies fill and float;
And, lilting where the laver lingers,
The starfish trips on all her fingers;
Where, 'neath his myriad spines ashock,
The sea-egg ripples down the rock;
An orange wonder daily guessed,
From darkness where the cuttles rest,
Moored o'er the darker deeps that hide
The blind white sea-snake and his bride
Who, drowsing, nose the long-lost ships
Let down through darkness to their lips.

A Matter of Fact.

There's a convict more in the Central Jail,
Behind the old mud wall;
There's a lifter less on the Border trail,
And the Queen's peace over all,
Dear boys,
The Queen's peace over all!

122

For we must bear our leader's blame,
On us the shame will fall,
If we lift our hand from a fettered land
And the Queen's peace over all,
Dear boys,
The Queen's peace over all!

The Lost Legion.

'Less you want your toes trod off you'd better get back at once,
For the bullocks are walking two by two,
The *byles* are walking two by two,
And the elephants bring the guns.
Ho! Yuss!
Great—big—long—black—forty-pounder guns:
Jiggery-jolty to and fro,
Each as big as a launch in tow—
Blind—dumb—broad-breeched—beggars o' battering-guns.

My Lord the Elephant.

All the world over, nursing their scars,
Sit the old fighting-men broke in the wars—
Sit the old fighting men, surly and grim
Mocking the lilt of the conquerors' hymn.

Dust of the battle o'erwhelmed them and hid.
Fame never found them for aught that they did.
Wounded and spent to the lazar they drew,
Lining the road where the Legions roll through.

Sons of the Laurel who press to your meed,
(Worthy God's pity most—ye who succeed!)
Ere you go triumphing, crowned, to the stars,
Pity poor fighting men, broke in the wars!

Collected.

SONG OF THE FIFTH RIVER

When first by Eden Tree,
The Four Great Rivers ran,
To each was appointed a Man
Her Prince and Ruler to be.

But after this was ordained,
(The ancient legends tell),
There came dark Israel,
For whom no River remained.

Then He Whom the Rivers obey
Said to him: 'Fling on the ground
A handful of yellow clay,
And a Fifth Great River shall run,
Mightier than these Four,
In secret the Earth around;
And Her secret evermore,
Shall be shown to thee and thy Race.'
So it was said and done.
And deep in the veins of Earth,
And, fed by a thousand springs
That comfort the market-place,
Or sap the power of Kings,

The Fifth Great River had birth,
Even as it was foretold—
The Secret River of Gold!

And Israel laid down
His sceptre and his crown,
To brood on that River's bank,
Where the waters flashed and sank,
And burrowed in earth and fell,
And bided a season below,
For reason that none might know,
Save only Israel.

He is Lord of the Last—
The Fifth, most wonderful, Flood.
He hears Her thunder past
And Her Song is in his blood.
He can foresay: 'She will fall,'
For he knows which fountain dries.
Behind which desert-belt
A thousand leagues to the South.

He can foresay: 'She will rise.'
He knows what far snows melt;
Along what mountain-wall
A thousand leagues to the North.
He snuffs the coming drouth
As he snuffs the coming rain,
He knows what each will bring forths
And turns it to his gain.

A Ruler without a Throne,
A Prince without a Sword,
Israel follows his quest.
In every land a guest,
Of many lands a lord,
In no land King is he.
But the Fifth Great River keeps
The secret of Her deeps
For Israel alone,
As it was ordered to be.

THE CHILDREN'S SONG

Land of our Birth, we pledge to thee
Our love and toil in the years to be;
When we are grown and take our place,
As men and women with our race.

Father in Heaven who lovest all,
Oh help Thy children when they call;
That they may build from age to age,
An undefilèd heritage.

Teach us to bear the yoke in youth,
With steadfastness and careful truth;
That, in our time, Thy Grace may give
The Truth whereby the Nations live.

Teach us to rule ourselves alway,
Controlled and cleanly night and day;
That we may bring, if need arise.
No maimed or worthless sacrifice.

Teach us to look in all our ends,
On Thee for judge, and not our friends;
That we, with Thee, may walk uncowed
By fear or favour of the crowd.

Teach us the Strength that cannot seek,
By deed or thought, to hurt the weak;
That, under Thee, we may possess
Man's strength to comfort man's distress.

Teach us Delight in simple things,
And Mirth that has no bitter springs;
Forgiveness free of evil done,
And Love to all men 'neath the sun!

Land of our Birth, our faith, our pride,
For whose dear sake our fathers died;
O Motherland, we pledge to thee,
Head, heart, and hand through the years to be!

PARADE-SONG OF THE CAMP-ANIMALS

ELEPHANTS OF THE GUN-TEAMS

We lent to Alexander the strength of Hercules,
The wisdom of our foreheads, the cunning of our knees.
We bowed our necks to service; they ne'er were loosed again,—
Make way there, way for the ten-foot teams
      Of the Forty-Pounder train!

GUN-BULLOCKS

Those heroes in their harnesses avoid a cannon-ball,
And what they know of powder upsets them one and all;
Then *we* come into action and tug the guns again,—
Make way there, way for the twenty yoke
      Of the Forty-Pounder train!

CAVALRY HORSES

By the brand on my withers, the finest of tunes
Is played by the Lancers, Hussars, and Dragoons,
And it's sweeter than 'Stables' or 'Water' to me.
The Cavalry Canter of 'Bonnie Dundee'!

Then feed us and break us and handle and groom,
And give us good riders and plenty of room,

130

And launch us in column of squadron and see
The Way of the War-horse to 'Bonnie Dundee'!

SCREW-GUN MULES

As me and my companions were scrambling up a hill,
The path was lost in rolling stones, but we went forward still;
For we can wriggle and climb, my lads, and turn up everywhere,
And it's our delight on a mountain height, with a leg or two to spare!

Good luck to every sergeant, then, that lets us pick our road!
Bad luck to all the driver-men that cannot pack a load!
For we can wriggle and climb, my lads, and turn up everywhere,
And it's our delight on a mountain height, with a leg or two to spare!

COMMISSARIAT CAMELS

We haven't a camelty tune of our own
To help us trollop along,
But every neck is a hair-trombone
(*Rtt-ta-ta-ta*! is a hair-trombone!)
And this is our marching-song:
Can't! Don't! Shan't! Won't!
Pass it along the line!
Somebody's pack has slid from his back,
'Wish it were only mine!
Somebody's load has tipped off in the road—
Cheer for a halt and a row!
Urrr! Yarrh! Grr! Arrh!
Somebody's catching it now!

ALL THE BEASTS TOGETHER

Children of the Camp are we,
Serving each in his degree;
Children of the yoke and goad,
Pack and harness, pad and load.
See our line across the plain.
Like a heel-rope bent again,
Beaching, writhing, rolling far.
Sweeping all away to war!
While the men that walk beside,
Dusty, silent, heavy-eyed,
Cannot tell why we or they
March and suffer day by day.

> *Children of the Camp are we,*
> *Serving each in hiss degree;*
> *Children of the yoke and goad,*
> *Pack and harness, pad and load.*

IF—

If you can keep your head when all about you
    Are losing theirs and blaming it on you;
If you can trust yourself when all men doubt you,
    But make allowance for their doubting too;
If you can wait and not be tired by waiting,
    Or being lied about, don't deal in lies,
Or being hated don't give way to hating,
    And yet don't look too good, nor talk too wise:

If you can dream—and not make dreams your master;
    If you can think—and not make thoughts your aim;
If you can meet with Triumph and Disaster
    And treat those two impostors just the same;
If you can bear to hear the truth you've spoken
    Twisted by knaves to make a trap for fools,
Or watch the things you gave your life to, broken,
    And stoop and build 'em up with worn-out tools:

If you can make one heap of all your winnings
    And risk it on one turn of pitch-and-toss,
And lose, and start again at your beginnings
    And never breathe a word about your loss;
If you can force your heart and nerve and sinew
    To serve your turn long after they are gone.

And so hold on when there is nothing in you
    Except the Will which says to them: 'Hold on!'

If you can talk with crowds and keep your virtue,
    Or walk with Kings—nor lose the common touch;
If neither foes nor loving friends can hurt you,
    If all men count with you, but none too much;
If you can fill the unforgiving minute
    With sixty seconds' worth of distance run,
Yours is the Earth and everything that's in it,
    And—which is more—you'll be a Man, my son!

THE PRODIGAL SON

(Western Version)

Here come I to my own again,
Fed, forgiven and known again,
Claimed by bone of my bone again
And cheered by flesh of my flesh.
The fatted calf is dressed for me,
But the husks have greater zest for me,
I think my pigs will be best for me,
So I'm off to the Yards afresh.

I never was very refined, you see,
(And it weighs on my brother's mind, you see)
But there's no reproach among swine, d'you see,
For being a bit of a swine.
So I'm off with wallet and staff to eat
The bread that is three parts chaff to wheat,
But glory be!—there's a laugh to it,
Which isn't the case when we dine.

My father glooms and advises me,
My brother sulks and despises me,
And Mother catechises me
Till I want to go out and swear.
And, in spite of the butler's gravity,

I know that the servants have it I
Am a monster of moral depravity,
And I'm damned if I think it's fair!

I wasted my substance, I know I did,
On riotous living, so I did,
But there's nothing on record to show I did
Worse than my betters have done.
They talk of the money I spent out there—
They hint at the pace that I went out there—
But they all forget I was sent out there
Alone as a rich man's son.

So I was a mark for plunder at once,
And lost my cash (can you wonder?) at once,
But I didn't give up and knock under at once,
I worked in the Yards, for a spell.
Where I spent my nights and my days with hogs,
And shared their milk and maize with hogs,
Till, I guess, I have learned what pays with hogs
And—I have that knowledge to sell!

So back I go to my job again,
Not so easy to rob again,
Or quite so ready to sob again
On any neck that's around.
I'm leaving, Pater. Goodbye to you!
God bless you, Mater! I'll write to you . . .
I wouldn't be impolite to you,
But, Brother, you *are* a hound!

THE NECESSITARIAN

I know not in Whose hands are laid
    To empty upon earth
From unsuspected ambuscade
    The very Urns of Mirth;

Who bids the Heavenly Lark arise
    And cheer our solemn round—
The Jest beheld with streaming eyes
    And grovellings on the ground;

Who joins the flats of Time and Chance
    Behind the prey preferred,
And thrones on Shrieking Circumstance
    The Sacredly Absurd,

Till Laughter, voiceless through excess,
    Waves mute appeal and sore,
Above the midriff's deep distress,
    For breath to laugh once more.

No creed hath dared to hail Him Lord,
    No raptured choirs proclaim,
And Nature's strenuous Overword
    Hath nowhere breathed His Name.

Yet, it must be, on wayside jape,
    The selfsame Power bestows
The selfsame power as went to shape
    His Planet or His Rose.

THE JESTER

There are three degrees of bliss
At the foot of Allah's Throne,
And the highest place is his
Who saves a brother's soul
At peril of his own.
There is the Power made known!

There are three degrees of bliss
In the Gardens of Paradise,
And the second place is his
Who saves his brother's soul
By excellent advice.
For there the Glory lies!

There are three degrees of bliss
And three abodes of the Blest,
And the lowest place is his
Who has saved a soul by a jest
And a brother's soul in sport . . .
But there do the Angels resort!

A SONG OF TRAVEL

Where's the lamp that Hero lit
    Once to call Leander home?
Equal Time hath shovelled it
    'Neath the wrack of Greece and Rome.
Neither wait we any more
That worn sail which Argo bore.

Dust and dust of ashes close
    All the Vestal Virgins' care;
And the oldest altar shows
    But an older darkness there.
Age-encamped Oblivion
Tenteth every light that shone!

Yet shall we, for Suns that die,
    Wall our wanderings from desire?
Or, because the Moon is high.
    Scorn to use a nearer fire?
Lest some envious Pharaoh stir,
Make our lives our sepulchre?

Nay! Though Time with petty Fate
    Prison us and Emperors,
By our Arts do we create
    That which Time himself devours—

Such machines as well may run
'Gainst the horses of the Sun.

When we would a new abode,
    Space, our tyrant King no more,
Lays the long lance of the road
    At our feet and flees before,
Breathless, ere we overwhelm,
    To submit a further realm!

THE TWO-SIDED MAN

Much I owe to the Land that grew—
More to the Life that fed—
But most to Allah Who gave me two
Separate sides to my head.

Much I reflect on the Good and the True
In the Faiths beneath the sun,
But most upon Allah Who gave me two
Sides to my head, not one.

Wesley's following, Calvin's flock,
White or yellow or bronze,
Shaman, Ju-ju or Angekok,
Minister, Mukamuk, Bonze—

Here is a health, my brothers, to you,
However your prayers are said,
And praised be Allah Who gave me two
Separate sides to my head!

I would go without shirt or shoe,
Friend, tobacco or bread,
Sooner than lose for a minute the two
Separate sides of my head!

142

'LUKANNON'

(Song of the breeding Seal. Aleutian Islands)

I met my mates in the morning (and oh, but I am old!)
Where roaring on the ledges the summer ground-swell rolled.
I heard them lift the chorus that drowned the breakers' song—
The Beaches of Lukannon—two million voices strong!

The song of pleasant stations beside the salt lagoons,
The song of blowing squadrons that shuffled down the dunes,
The song of midnight dances that churned the sea to flame—
The Beaches of Lukannon—before the sealers came!

I met my mates in the morning (I'll never meet them more!);
They came and went in legions that darkened all the shore.
And through the foam-flecked offing as far as voice could reach
We hailed the landing-parties and we sang them up the beach.

The Beaches of Lukannon—the winter-wheat so tall—
The dripping, crinkled lichens, and the sea-fog drenching all!
The platforms of our playground, all shining smooth and worn!
The Beaches of Lukannon—the home where we were born!

I meet my mates in the morning, a broken, scattered band.
Men shoot us in the water and club us on the land;
Men drive us to the Salt House like silly sheep and tame,
And still we sing Lukannon—before the sealers came.

Wheel down, wheel down to southward! Oh, Gooverooska go!
And tell the Deep-Sea Viceroys the story of our woe;
Ere, empty as the shark's egg the tempest flings ashore,
The Beaches of Lukannon shall know their sons no more!

AN ASTROLOGER'S SONG

To the Heavens above us
    O look and behold
The Planets that love us
    All harnessed in gold!
What chariots, what horses,
    Against us shall bide
While the Stars in their courses
    Do fight on our side?

All thought, all desires,
    That are under the sun,
Are one with their fires,
    As we also are one.
All matter, all spirit,
    All fashion, all frame,
Receive and inherit
    Their strength from the same.

Oh, man that deniest
    All power save thine own,
Their power in the highest
    Is mightily shown.
Not less in the lowest
    That power is made clear

(Oh, man, if thou knowest,
    What treasure is here!)

Earth quakes in her throes
    And we wonder for why.
But the blind planet knows
    When her ruler is nigh;
And, attuned since Creation
    To perfect accord,
She thrills in her station
    And yearns to her Lord.

The waters have risen,
    The springs are unbound—
The floods break their prison,
    And ravin around.
No rampart withstands 'em,
    Their fury will last,
Till the Sign that commands 'em
    Sinks low or swings past.

Through abysses unproven,
    O'er gulfs beyond thought,
Our portion is woven,
    Our burden is brought.
Yet They that prepare it,
    Whose Nature we share,
Make us who must bear it
    Well able to bear.

Though terrors o'ertake us
 We'll not be afraid.
No Power can unmake us
 Save that which has made.
Nor yet beyond reason
 Or hope shall we fall—
All things have their season,
 And Mercy crowns all!

Then, doubt not, ye fearful—
 The Eternal is King—
Up, heart, and be cheerful,
 And lustily sing:—
What chariots, what horses,
 Against us shall bide
While the Stars in their courses
 Do fight on our side?

'THE POWER OF THE DOG'

There is sorrow enough in the natural way
From men and women to fill our day;
But when we are certain of sorrow in store,
Why do we always arrange for more?
Brothers and Sisters, I bid you beware
Of giving your heart to a dog to tear.

Buy a pup and your money will buy
Love unflinching that cannot lie—
Perfect passion and worship fed
By a kick in the ribs or a pat on the head.
Nevertheless it is hardly fair
To risk your heart for a dog to tear.

When the fourteen years which Nature permits
Are closing in asthma, or tumour, or fits,
And the vet's unspoken prescription runs
To lethal chambers or loaded guns,
Then you will find—it's your own affair,
But . . . you've given your heart to a dog to tear.

When the body that lived at your single will,
When the whimper of welcome is stilled (how still!),
When the spirit that answered your every mood
Is gone—wherever it goes—for good,

You will discover how much you care,
And will give your heart to a dog to tear.

We've sorrow enough in the natural way,
When it comes to burying Christian clay.
Our loves are not given, but only lent,
At compound interest of cent per cent.
Though it is not always the case, I believe,
That the longer we've kept 'em, the more do we grieve:
For, when debts are payable, right or wrong,
A short-time loan is as bad as a long—
So why in—Heaven (before we are there)
Should we give our hearts to a dog to tear?

THE RABBI'S SONG

If Thought can reach to Heaven,
    On Heaven let it dwell,
For fear thy Thought be given
    Like power to reach to Hell.
For fear the desolation
    And darkness of thy mind
Perplex an habitation
    Which thou hast left behind.

Let nothing linger after—
    No whimpering ghost remain,
In wall, or beam, or rafter,
    Of any hate or pain.
Cleanse and call home thy spirit,
    Deny her leave to cast,
On aught thy heirs inherit,
    The shadow of her past.
For think, in all thy sadness,
    What road our griefs may take;
Whose brain reflect our madness,
    Or whom our terrors shake.
For think, lest any languish
    By cause of thy distress—
The arrows of our anguish
    Fly farther than we guess.

Our lives, our tears, as water,
    Are spilled upon the ground;
God giveth no man quarter,
    Yet God a means hath found,
Though faith and hope have vanished,
    And even love grows dim—
A means whereby His banished
    Be not expelled from Him.

THE BEE BOY'S SONG

Bees! Bees! Hark to your bees!
'Hide from your neighbours as much as you please,
But all that has happened, to us you must tell,
Or else we will give you no honey to sell!'

A maiden in her glory,
    Upon her wedding-day,
Must tell her Bees the story,
    Or else they'll fly away.
        Fly away—die away—
            Dwindle down and leave you!
            But if you don't deceive your Bees,
                Your Bees will not deceive you.

Marriage, birth or buryin',
    News across the seas,
All you're sad or merry in,
    You must tell the Bees.
        Tell 'em coming in an' out,
            Where the Fanners fan,
        'Cause the Bees are just about
            As curious as a man!

Don't you wait where trees are,
    When the lightnings play,

Nor don't you hate where Bees are,
    Or else they'll pine away.
        Pine away—dwine away—
            Anything to leave you!
        But if you never grieve your Bees,
            Your Bees'll never grieve you.

THE RETURN OF THE CHILDREN

Neither the harps nor the crowns amused, nor the cherubs' dove-winged
  races—
Holding hands forlornly the Children wandered beneath the Dome,
Plucking the splendid robes of the passers-by, and with pitiful faces
Begging what Princes and Powers refused:—'Ah, please will you let us
  go home?'

Over the jewelled floor, nigh weeping, ran to them Mary the Mother,
Kneeled and caressed and made promise with kisses, and drew them
  along to the gateway—
Yea, the all-iron unbribeable Door which Peter must guard and none other.
Straightway She took the Keys from his keeping, and opened and freed
  them straightway.

Then, to Her Son, Who had seen and smiled, She said: 'On the night that
  I bore Thee,
What didst Thou care for a love beyond mine or a heaven that was not
  my arm?
Didst Thou push from the nipple, O Child, to hear the angels adore Thee?
When we two lay in the breath of the kine?' And He said:—'Thou hast
  done no harm.'

So through the Void the Children ran homeward merrily hand in hand,
Looking neither to left nor right where the breathless Heavens stood
    still.
And the Guards of the Void resheathed their swords, for they heard the
    Command:
'Shall I that have suffered the children to come to Me hold them against
    their will?'

MERROW DOWN

I

There runs a road by Merrow Down—
    A grassy track today it is—
An hour out of Guildford town,
    Above the river Wey it is.

Here, when they heard the horse-bells ring,
    The ancient Britons dressed and rode
To watch the dark Phoenicians bring
    Their goods along the Western Road.

Yes, here, or hereabouts, they met
    To hold their racial talks and such—
To barter beads for Whitby jet,
    And tin for gay shell torques and such.

But long and long before that time
    (When bison used to roam on it)
Did Taffy and her Daddy climb
    That Down, and had their home on it.

Then beavers built in Broadstonebrook
    And made a swamp where Bramley stands;
And bears from Shere would come and look
    For Taffimai where Shamley stands.

The Wey, that Taffy called Wagai,
　　Was more than six times bigger then;
And all the Tribe of Tegumai
　　They cut a noble figure then!

II

Of all the Tribe of Tegumai
　　Who cut that figure, none remain,—
On Merrow Down the cuckoos cry—
　　The silence and the sun remain.

But as the faithful years return
　　And hearts unwounded sing again,
Comes Taffy dancing through the fern
　　To lead the Surrey spring again.

Her brows are bound with bracken-fronds,
　　And golden elf-locks fly above;
Her eyes are bright as diamonds
　　And bluer than the sky above.

In mocassins and deer-skin cloak,
　　Unfearing, free and fair she flits,
And lights her little damp-wood smoke
　　To show her Daddy where she flits.

For far—oh, very far behind,
　　So far she cannot call to him,
Comes Tegumai alone to find
　　The daughter that was all to him.

OLD MOTHER LAIDINWOOL

'Old Mother Laidinwool had nigh twelve months been dead.
She heard the hops was doing well, an' so popped up her head,'
For said she: 'The lads I've picked with when I was young and fair,
They're bound to be at hopping and I'm bound to meet 'em there!'

Let me up and go
Back to the work I know, Lord!
Back to the work I know, Lord!
For it's dark where I lie down, My Lord!
An' it's dark where I lie down!

Old Mother Laidinwool, she give her bones a shake,
An' trotted down the churchyard path as fast as she could make.
She met the Parson walking, but she says to him, says she:
'Oh don't let no one trouble for a poor old ghost like me!'

'Twas all a warm September an' the hops had flourished grand,
She saw the folks get into 'em with stockin's on their hands;
An' none of 'em was foreigners but all which she had known,
And old Mother Laidinwool she blessed 'em every one.

She saw her daughters picking, an' their children them beside,
An' she moved among the babies an' she stilled 'em when they cried.
She saw their clothes was bought, not begged, an' they was clean an' fat,
An' old Mother Laidinwool she thanked the Lord for that.

Old Mother Laidinwool she waited on all day
Until it come too dark to see an' people went away—
Until it come too dark to see an' lights began to show,
An' old Mother Laidinwool she hadn't where to go.

Old Mother Laidinwool she give her bones a shake,
An' trotted back to churchyard-mould as fast as she could make.
She went where she was bidden to an' there laid down her ghost, . . .
An' the Lord have mercy on you in the Day you need it most!

Let me in again,
Out of the wet an' rain, Lord!
Out of the dark an rain, Lord!
For it's best as you shall say, My Lord!
An' it's best as you shall say!

CHAPTER HEADINGS

JUST-SO STORIES

When the cabin port-holes are dark and green
    Because of the seas outside;
When the ship goes *wop* (with a wiggle between)
And the steward falls into the soup-tureen,
    And the trunks begin to slide;
When Nursey lies on the floor in a heap,
And Mummy tells you to let her sleep,
And you aren't waked or washed or dressed,
Why, then you will know (if you haven't guessed)
You're 'Fifty North and Forty West!'

How the Whale got his Throat.

The Camel's hump is an ugly lump
    Which well you may see at the Zoo;
But uglier yet is the hump we get
    From having too little to do.

Kiddies and grown-ups too-oo-oo,
If we haven't enough to do-oo-oo.
      We get the hump—
      Cameelious hump—
The hump that is black and blue!

We climb out of bed with a frouzly head
    And a snarly-yarly voice.
We shiver and scowl and we grunt and we growl
    At our bath and our boots and our toys;

And there ought to be a corner for me
(And I know there is one for you)
      When we get the hump—
      Cameelious hump—
The hump that is black and blue!

The cure for this ill is not to sit still,
    Or frowst with a book by the fire;
But to take a large hoe and a shovel also,
    And dig till you gently perspire;

And then you will find that the sun and the wind,
And the Djinn of the Garden too,
      Have lifted the hump—
      The horrible hump—
The hump that is black and blue!

I get it as well as you-oo-oo—
If I haven't enough to do-oo-oo!
      We all get hump—
      Cameelious hump—
Kiddies and grown-ups too!

    How the Camel got his Hump.

I am the Most Wise Baviaan, saying in most wise tones,
'Let us melt into the landscape—just us two by our lones.'
People have come—in a carriage—calling. But Mummy is there . . .
Yes, I can go if you take me—Nurse says *she* don't care.
Let's go up to the pig-styes and sit on the farmyard rails!
Let's say things to the bunnies, and watch 'em skitter their tails!
Let's—oh, *anything*, daddy, so long as it's you and me,
And going truly exploring, and not being in till tea!
Here's your boots (I've brought 'em), and here's your cap and stick,
And here's your pipe and tobacco. Oh, come along out of it—quick!

How the Leopard got his Spots.

I keep six honest serving-men
    (They taught me all I knew);
Their names are What and Why and When
    And How and Where and Who.
I send them over land and sea,
    I send them east and west;
But after they have worked for me,
    I give them all a rest.

I let them rest from nine till five,
    For I am busy then,
As well as breakfast, lunch, and tea,
    For they are hungry men.

But different folk have different views;
    I know a person small—
She keeps ten million serving-men,
    Who get no rest at all!

She sends 'em abroad on her own affairs,
    From the second she opens her eyes—
One million Hows, two million Wheres,
    And seven million Whys!

The Elephant's Child.

This is the mouth-filling song of the race that was run by a Boomer.
Run in a single burst—only event of its kind—
Started by Big God Nqong from Warrigaborrigarooma,
Old Man Kangaroo first, Yellow-Dog Dingo behind.

Kangaroo bounded away, his back-legs working like pistons—
Bounded from morning till dark, twenty-five feet at a bound.
Yellow-Dog Dingo lay like a yellow cloud in the distance—
Much too busy to bark. My! but they covered the ground!

Nobody knows where they went, or followed the track that they flew in,
For that Continent hadn't been given a name.
They ran thirty degrees, from Torres Straits to the Leeuwin
(Look at the Atlas, please), then they ran back as they came.

S'posing you could trot from Adelaide to the Pacific,
For an afternoon's run—half what these gentlemen did—
You would feel rather hot, but your legs would develop terrific—
Yes, my importunate son, you'd be a Marvellous Kid!

The Sing-Song of Old Man Kangaroo.

I've never sailed the Amazon,
  I've never reached Brazil;
But the *Don* and *Magdalena*,
  They can go there when they will!

        Yes, weekly from Southampton,
        Great steamers, white and gold,
        Go rolling down to Rio
        (Roll down—roll down to Rio!).
        And I'd like to roll to Rio
        Some day before I'm old!

I've never seen a Jaguar,
  Nor yet an Armadill—
O dilloing in his armour,
  And I s'pose I never will,

        Unless I go to Rio
        These wonders to behold—
        Roll down—roll down to Rio—
        Roll really down to Rio!
        Oh, I'd love to roll to Rio
        Some day before I'm old!

        The Beginning of the Armadilloes.

China-going P. and O.'s
Pass Pau Amma's playground close,
And his Pusat Tasek lies
Near the track of most B.I.'s.
N.Y.K. and N.D.L.
Know Pau Amma's home as well

As the Fisher of the Sea knows
'Bens,' M.M.'s, and Rubattinos.
But (and this is rather queer)
A.T.L.'s can *not* come here;
O. and O. and D.O.A.
Must go round another way.
Orient, Anchor, Bibby, Hall,
Never go that way at all.
U.C.S. would have a fit
If it found itself on it.
And if 'Beavers' took their cargoes
To Penang instead of Lagos,
Or a fat Shaw-Savill bore
Passengers to Singapore,
Or a White Star were to try a
Little trip to Sourabaya,
Or a B.S.A. went on
Past Natal to Cheribon,
Then great Mr. Lloyds would come
With a wire and drag them home!

* * * * *

You'll know what my riddle means
When you've eaten mangosteens.

The Crab that Played with the Sea.

Pussy can sit by the fire and sing,
    Pussy can climb a tree,
Or play with a silly old cork and string
    To 'muse herself, not me.

But *I* like *Binkie* my dog, because
    He knows how to behave;
So, *Binkie's* the same as the First Friend was,
    And I am the Man in the Cave!

Pussy will play man-Friday till
    It's time to wet her paw
And make her walk on the window-sill
    (For the footprint Crusoe saw);
Then she fluffles her tail and mews,
    And scratches and won't attend.
But *Binkie* will play whatever I choose,
    And he is my true First Friend!

Pussy will rub my knees with her head
    Pretending she loves me hard;
But the very minute I go to my bed
    Pussy runs out in the yard,
And there she stays till the morning-light;
    So I know it is only pretend;
But *Binkie*, he snores at my feet all night,
    And he is my Firstest Friend!

The Cat that Walked by Himself

There was never a Queen like Balkis,
    From here to the wide world's end;
But Balkis talked to a butterfly
    As you would talk to a friend.

There was never a King like Solomon,
    Not since the world began;
But Solomon talked to a butterfly
    As a man would talk to a man.

She was Queen of Sabæa—
    And *he* was Asia's Lord—
But they both of 'em talked to butterflies
    When they took their walks abroad!

    The Butterfly that Stamped.

THE LOOKING-GLASS

(A Country Dance)

Queen Bess was Harry's daughter. Stand forward partners all!
She danced King Philip down-a down,
And left her shoe to show 'twas true—
> *(The very tune I'm playing you)*
In Norgem at Brickwall!

The Queen was in her chamber, and she was middling old,
Her petticoat was satin, and her stomacher was gold.
Backwards and forwards and sideways did she pass,
Making up her mind to face the cruel looking-glass.
The cruel looking-glass that will never show a lass
As comely or as kindly or as young as what she was!

Queen Bess was Harry's daughter. Now hand your partners all!
The Queen was in her chamber, a-combing of her hair.
There came Queen Mary's spirit and It stood behind her chair.
Singing, 'Backwards and forwards and sideways may you pass,
But I will stand behind you till you face the looking-glass.
The cruel looking-glass that will never show a lass
As lovely or unlucky or as lonely as I was!'

Queen Bess was Harry's daughter.—Now turn your partners all!
The Queen was in her chamber, a-weeping very sore.

There came Lord Leicester's spirit and It scratched upon the door,
Singing, 'Backwards and forwards and sideways may you pass,
But I will walk beside you till you face the looking-glass.
The cruel looking-glass that will never show a lass
As hard and unforgiving or as wicked as you was!'

Queen Bess was Harry's daughter. Now kiss your partners all!

The Queen was in her chamber; her sins were on her head.
She looked the spirits up and down and statelily she said:—
Backwards and forwards and sideways though I've been,
Yet I am Harry's daughter and I am England's Queen!'
And she faced the looking-glass (and whatever else there was),
And she saw her day was over and she saw her beauty pass
In the cruel looking-glass, that can always hurt a lass
More hard than any ghost there is or any man there was!

THE QUEEN'S MEN

Valour and Innocence
Have latterly gone hence
To certain death by certain shame attended.
Envy—ah! even to tears!—
The fortune of their years
Which, though so few, yet so divinely ended.

Scarce had they lifted up
Life's full and fiery cup,
Than they had set it down untouched before them.
Before their day arose
They beckoned it to close—
Close in confusion and destruction o'er them.

They did not stay to ask
What prize should crown their task,
Well sure that prize was such as no man strives for;
But passed into eclipse,
Her kiss upon their lips—
Even Belphoebe's, whom they gave their lives for!

THE CITY OF SLEEP

Over the edge of the purple down,
   Where the single lamplight gleams.
Know ye the road to the Merciful Town
   That is hard by the Sea of Dreams—
Where the poor may lay their wrongs away,
   And the sick may forget to-weep?
But we—pity us! Oh, pity us!
   We wakeful; ah, pity us!—
We must go back with Policeman Day—
   Back from the City of Sleep!

Weary they turn from the scroll and crown,
   Fetter and prayer and plough—
They that go up to the Merciful Town,
   For her gates are closing now.
It is their right in the Baths of Night
   Body and soul to steep,
But we—pity us! ah, pity us!
   We wakeful; oh, pity us!—
We must go back with Policeman Day—
   Back from the City of Sleep!

Over the edge of the purple down,
        Ere the tender dreams begin,
Look—we may look—at the Merciful Towns
        But we may not enter in!
Outcasts all, from her guarded wall
        Back to our watch we creep:
We—pity us! ah, pity us!
        We wakeful; oh, pity us!—
We that go back with Policeman Day—
        Back from the City of Sleep!

THE WIDOWER

For a season there must be pain—
For a little, little space
I shall lose the sight of her face,
Take back the old life again
While She is at rest in her place.

For a season this pain must endure—
For a little, little while
I shall sigh more often than smile,
Till Time shall work me a cure,
And the pitiful days beguile.

For that season we must be apart,
For a little length of years,
Till my life's last hour nears,
And, above the beat of my heart,
I hear Her voice in my ears.

But I shall not understand—
Being set on some later love,
Shall not know her for whom I strove,
Till she reach me forth her hand,
Saying, 'Who but I have the right?'
And out of a troubled night
Shall draw me safe to the land.

THE PRAYER OF MIRIAM COHEN

From the wheel and the drift of Things
Deliver us, Good Lord,
And we will face the wrath of Kings,
The faggot and the sword!

Lay not Thy Works before our eyes,
Nor vex us with Thy Wars,
Lest we should feel the straining skies
O'ertrod by trampling stars.

Hold us secure behind the gates
Of saving flesh and bone,
Lest we should dream what dream awaits
The soul escaped alone.

Thy Path, Thy Purposes conceal
From our beleaguered realm,
Lest any shattering whisper steal
Upon us and o'erwhelm.

A veil 'twixt us and Thee, Good Lord,
A veil 'twixt us and Thee,
Lest we should hear too clear, too clear,
And unto madness see!

THE SONG OF THE LITTLE HUNTER

Ere Mor the Peacock flutters, ere the Monkey People cry,
    Ere Chil the Kite swoops down a furlong sheer,
Through the Jungle very softly flits a shadow and a sigh—
    He is Fear, O Little Hunter, he is Fear!
Very softly down the glade runs a waiting, watching shade,
    And the whisper spreads and widens far and near.
And the sweat is on thy brow, for he passes even now—
    He is Fear, O Little Hunter, he is Fear!

Ere the moon has climbed the mountain, ere the rocks are ribbed with
    light,
    When the downward-dipping trails are dank and drear,

Comes a breathing hard behind thee—*snuffle-snuffle* through the night—
    It is Fear, O Little Hunter, it is Fear!
On thy knees and draw the bow; bid the shrilling arrow go;
    In the empty, mocking thicket plunge the spear!
But thy hands are loosed and weak, and the blood has left thy cheek—
    It is Fear, O Little Hunter, it is Fear!

When the heat-cloud sucks the tempest, when the slivered pine-trees fall,
    When the blinding, blaring rain-squalls lash and veer,
Through the war-gongs of the thunder rings a voice more loud than all—
    It is Fear, O Little Hunter, it is Fear!

Now the spates are banked and deep; now the footless boulders leap—
    Now the lightning shows each littlest leaf-rib clear—
But thy throat is shut and dried, and thy heart against thy side
    Hammers: Fear, O Little Hunter—this is Fear!

GOW'S WATCH

ACT II. SCENE 2

The pavilion in the Gardens. Enter Ferdinand and the King

Ferdinand. Your tiercel's too long at hack. Sir.
He's no eyass
But a passage-hawk that footed ere we caught him.
Dangerously free o' the air. Faith, were he mine
(As mine's the glove he binds to for his tirings)
I'd fly him with a make-hawk. He's in yarak
Plumed to the very point. So manned, so weathered!
Give him the firmament God made him for.
And what shall take the air of him?

The King. A young wing yet.
Bold—overbold on the perch, but, think you,
Ferdinand,
He can endure the tall skies yonder? Cozen
Advantage out of the teeth of the hurricane?
Choose his own mate against the lammer-geier?
Ride out a night-long tempest, hold his pitch
Between the lightning and the cloud it leaps from,
Never too pressed to kill?

Ferdinand. I'll answer for him.
Bating all parable, I know the Prince.
There's a bleak devil in the young, my Lord;
God put it there to save 'em from their elders
And break their father's heart, but bear them scatheless
Through mire and thorns and blood if need be.
    Think
What our prime saw! Such glory, such achievements
As now our children, wondering at, examine
Themselves to see if they shall hardly equal.
But what cared we while we wrought the wonders?
     Nothing!
The rampant deed contented.

The King. Little enough, God knows! But afterwards? After—
There comes the reckoning. I would save him that.

Ferdinand. Save him dry scars that ache of winter-nights.
Worn out self-pity and as much of knowledge
As makes old men fear judgment? Then loose him—loose him,
A' God's name loose him to adventure early!
And trust some random pike, or half-backed horse,
Besides what's caught in Italy, to save him.

The King. I know. I know. And yet
. . . What stirs in the garden?

Enter Gow and a Gardener bearing the Prince's body

Ferdinand.(Gods give me patience!) Gow and a gardener
Bearing some load along in the dusk to the dunghill.
Nay—a dead branch—But as I said, the Prince—

178

The King. They've set it down. Strange that
they work so late.

Gow (setting down the body). Heark, you unsanctified
fool, while I set out our story. We found it, this side
the North park wall which it had climbed to pluck
nectarines from the alley. Heark again! There
was a nectarine in its hand when we found it, and
the naughty brick that slipped from the coping
beneath its foot and so caused its death, lies now
under the wall for the King to see.

The King (above). The King to see! Why should
he? Who's the man?

Gow. That is your tale. Swerve from it by so
much as the breadth of my dagger and here's your
instant reward. You heard not, saw not, and by the
Horns of ninefold-cuckolded Jupiter you thought not
nor dreamed not anything more or other!

The King. Ninefold-cuckolded Jupiter. That's a
rare oath! Shall we look closer?

Ferdinand. Not yet, my Lord! (I cannot hear him
breathe.)

Gardener. The North park wall? It was so.
Plucking nectarines. It shall be. But how shall
I say if any ask why our Lady the Queen—

Gow (stabs him). Thus! Hie after the Prince
and tell him y'are the first fruits of his nectarine
tree. Bleed there behind the laurels.

The King. Why did Gow buffet the clown?
What said he? I'll go look.

Ferdinand (above). Save yourself! It is the
King!

Enter the King and Ferdinand to Gow

Gow. God save you! This was the Prince!

The King. The Prince! Not a dead branch?
(Uncovers the face.)
My flesh and blood! My son! my son! my son!

Ferdinand (to Gow). I had feared something of
this. And that fool yonder?

Gow. Dead, or as good. He cannot speak.

Ferdinand. Better so.

The King. 'Loosed to adventure early!' Tell
the tale.

Gow. Saddest truth alack! I came upon him
not a half hour since, fallen from the North park
wall over against the Deerpark side—dead—dead!—a

180

nectarine in his hand that the dear lad must have
climbed for, and plucked the very instant, look you,
that a brick slipped on the coping. 'Tis there now.
So I lifted him, but his neck was as you see—and
already cold.

The King. Oh, very cold. But why should he
have troubled to climb? He was free of all the
fruit in my garden, God knows! . . . What, Gow?

Gow. Surely, God knows!

The King. A lad's trick. But I love him the
better for it . . . True, he's past loving . . . And
now we must tell our Queen. What a coil at the
day's end! She'll grieve for him. Not as I shall;
Ferdinand, but as youth for youth. They were
much of the same age. Playmate for playmate.
See, he wears her colours. That is the knot she
gave him last—last . . . Oh God! When was
yesterday?

Ferdinand. Come in! Come in, my Lord.
There's a dew falling.

The King. He'll take no harm of it. I'll follow presently . . .
He's all his mother's now and none of mine—
Her very face on the bride-pillow. Yet I tricked her.
But that was later—and she never guessed.
I do not think he sinned much—he's too young—
Much the same age as my Queen. God must not judge him

Too hardly for such slips as youth may fall in.
But I'll entreat that Throne.

(Prays by the body.)

Gow. The Heavens hold up still. Earth opens
not and this dew's mere water. What shall a man
think of it all? *(To Gardener.)* Not dead yet,
sirrah? I bade you follow the Prince. Despatch!

Gardener. Some kind soul pluck out the dagger.
Why did you slay me? I'd done no wrong. I'd ha'
kept it secret till my dying day. But not now—not
now! I'm dying. The Prince fell from the Queen's
chamber window. I saw it in the nut alley. He
was—

Ferdinand. But what made you in the nut alley
at that hour?

Gardener. No wrong. No more than another
man's wife. Jocasta of the still-room. She'd kissed
me goodnight too; but that's over with the
rest . . . I've stumbled on the Prince's beastly
loves, and I pay for all. Let me pass!

Gow. Count it your fortune, honest man. You
would have revealed it to your woman at the next
meeting. You fleshmongers are all one feather.
(Plucks out the dagger.)

182

Go in peace and lay your death to Fortune's door.
He's sped—thank Fortune!

Ferdinand. Who knows not Fortune, glutted on
easy thrones,
Stealing from feasts as rare to coney-catch
Privily in the hedgerows for a clown.
With that same cruel-lustful hand and eye,
Those nails and wedges, that one hammer and lead,
And the very gerb of long-stored lightning loosed.
Yesterday 'gainst some King.

The King. I have pursued with prayers where my heart warns me
My soul shall overtake—

Enter the Queen

The King. Look not! Wait till I tell you,
dearest . . . Air! . . .
'Loosed to adventure early'
. . . I go late. *(Dies.)*

Gow. So! God hath cut off the Prince in his
pleasures. Gow, to save the King, hath silenced one
poor fool who knew how it befell, and now the
King's dead, needs only that the Queen should kill
Gow and all's safe for her this side o' the Judgment.
. . . Senor Ferdinand, the wind's easterly. I'm for
the road.

Ferdinand. My horse is at the gate. God speed
you. Whither?

Gow. To the Duke, if the Queen does not lay
hands on me before. However it goes, I charge you
bear witness, Senor Ferdinand, I served the old
King faithfully. To the death, Senor Ferdinand—to
the death!

184

THE WISHING CAPS

Life's all getting and giving.
I've only myself to give.
What shall I do for a living?
I've only one life to live.
End it? I'll not find another.
Spend it? But how shall I best?
Sure the wise plan is to live like a man
And Luck may look after the rest!
Largesse! Largesse, Fortune!
Give or hold at your will.
If I've no care for Fortune,
Fortune must follow me still.

Bad Luck, she is never a lady,
But the commonest wench on the street,
Shuffling, shabby and shady,
Shameless to pass or meet.
Walk with her once—it's a weakness!
Talk to her twice—it's a crime!
Thrust her away when she gives you 'good day,'
And the besom won't board you next time.
Largesse! Largesse, Fortune!
What is Your Ladyship's mood?
If I've no care for Fortune,
My Fortune is bound to be good!

Good Luck, she is never a lady,
But the cursedest quean alive!
Tricksey, wincing and jady,
Kittle to lead or drive.
Greet her—she's hailing a stranger!
Meet her—she's busking to leave.
Let her alone for a shrew to the bone,
And the hussy comes plucking your sleeve!
Largesse! Largesse, Fortune!
I'll neither follow nor flee.
If I don't run after Fortune,
Fortune must run after me!

'BY THE HOOF OF THE WILD GOAT'

By the Hoof of the Wild Goat uptossed
From the cliff where she lay in the Sun
Fell the Stone
To the Tarn where the daylight is lost,
So she fell from the light of the Sun
And alone!

Now the fall was ordained from the first
With the Goat and the Cliff and the Tarn,
But the Stone
Knows only her life is accursed
As she sinks from the light of the Sun
And alone!

Oh Thou Who has builded the World,
Oh Thou Who has lighted the Sun,
Oh Thou Who has darkened the Tarn,
Judge Thou
The sin of the Stone that was hurled
By the goat from the light of the Sun,
As she sinks in the mire of the Tarn,
Even now—even now—even now!

SONG OF THE RED WAR-BOAT

(A.D. 683)

Shove off from the wharf-edge! Steady!
Watch for a smooth! Give way!
If she feels the lop already
She'll stand on her head in the bay.
It's ebb—it's dusk—it's blowing.
The shoals are a mile of white.
But (snatch her along!) we're going
To find our master tonight.

For we hold that in all disaster
Of shipwreck, storm, or sword,
A Man must stand by his Master
When once he has pledged his word.

Raging seas have we rowed in,
But we seldom saw them thus;
Our master is angry with Odin—
Odin is angry with us!
Heavy odds have we taken,
But never before such odds.
The Gods know they are forsaken,
We must risk the wrath of the Gods!

Over the crest she flies from,
Into its hollow she drops,
Cringes and clears her eyes from
The wind-torn breaker-tops,
Ere out on the shrieking shoulder
Of a hill-high surge she drives.
Meet her! Meet her and hold her!
Pull for your scoundrel lives!

The thunders bellow and clamour
The harm that they mean to do!
There goes Thor's own Hammer
Cracking the dark in two!
Close! But the blow has missed her,
Here comes the wind of the blow!
Row or the squall'll twist her
Broadside on to it!—*Row!*

Heark 'ee, Thor of the Thunder!
We are not here for a jest—
For wager, warfare, or plunder,
Or to put your power to test.
This work is none of our wishing—
We would house at home if we might—
But our master is wrecked out fishing.
We go to find him tonight.

For we hold that in all disaster—
As the Gods Themselves have said—
A Man must stand by his Master
Till one of the two is dead.

That is our way of thinking,
Now you can do as you will,
While we try to save her from sinking
And hold her head to it still.
Bale her and keep her moving,
Or she'll break her back in the trough . . .
Who said the weather's improving,
Or the swells are taking off?

Sodden, and chafed and aching,
Gone in the loins and knees—
No matter—the day is breaking,
And there's far less weight to the seas!
Up mast, and finish baling—
In oars, and out with the mead—
The rest will be two-reef sailing . . .
That was a night indeed!

But we hold that in all disaster
(And faith, we have found it true!)
If only you stand by your master,
The Gods will stand by you!

MORNING SONG IN THE JUNGLE

One moment past our bodies cast
　　No shadow on the plain;
Now clear and black they stride our track,
　　And we run home again.
In morning hush, each rock and bush
　　Stands hard, and high, and raw:
Then give the Call: *'Good rest to all*
　　That keep the Jungle Law!'

Now horn and pelt our peoples melt
　　In covert to abide;
Now, crouched and still, to cave and hill
　　Our Jungle Barons glide.
Now, stark and plain, Man's oxen strain,
　　That draw the new-yoked plough;
Now, stripped and dread, the dawn is red
　　Above the lit *talao*.

Ho! Get to lair! The sun's aflare
　　Behind the breathing grass:
And creaking through the young bamboo
　　The warning whispers pass.
By day made strange, the woods we range
　　With blinking eyes we scan;

While down the skies the wild duck cries:
  'The Day—the Day to Man!'

The dew is dried that drenched our hide,
    Or washed about our way;
And where we drank, the puddled bank
    Is crisping into clay.
The traitor Dark gives up each mark
    Of stretched or hooded claw;
Then hear the Call: *'Good rest to all*
    That keep the Jungle Law!'

BLUE ROSES

Roses red and roses white
Plucked I for my love's delight.
She would none of all my posies—
Bade me gather her blue roses.

Half the world I wandered through,
Seeking where such flowers grew;
Half the world unto my quest
Answered me with laugh and jest.

Home I came at wintertide,
But my silly love had died,
Seeking with her latest breath
Roses from the arms of Death.

It may be beyond the grave
She shall find what she would have.
Mine was but an idle quest—
Roses white and red are best.

A RIPPLE SONG

Once a ripple came to land
    In the golden sunset burning—
Lapped against a maiden's hand,
    By the ford returning.

Dainty foot and gentle breast—
Here, across, be glad and rest.
'Maiden, wait,' the ripple saith;
'Wait awhile, for I am Death!'

'Where my lover calls I go—
    Shame it were to treat him coldly—
'Twas a fish that circled so,
    Turning over boldly.'

Dainty foot and tender heart,
Wait the loaded ferry-cart.
'Wait, ah, wait!' the ripple saith;
'Maiden, wait, for I am Death!'

'When my lover calls I haste—
    Dame Disdain was never wedded!'
Ripple-ripple round her waist,
    Clear the current eddied.

Foolish heart and faithful hand,
Little feet that touched no land.
Far away the ripple sped,
Ripple—ripple—running red!

BUTTERFLIES

Eyes aloft, over dangerous places,
The children follow the butterflies,
And, in the sweat of their upturned faces,
Slash with a net at the empty skies.

So it goes they fall amid brambles,
And sting their toes on the nettle-tops,
Till, after a thousand scratches and scrambles,
They wipe their brows and the hunting stops.

Then to quiet them comes their father
And stills the riot of pain and grief,
Saying, 'Little ones, go and gather
Out of my garden a cabbage-leaf.

'You will find on it whorls and clots of
Dull grey eggs that, properly fed,
Turn, by way of the worm, to lots of
Glorious butterflies raised from the dead . . .,'

'Heaven is beautiful, Earth is ugly,'
The three-dimensioned preacher saith,
So we must not look where the snail and the slug lie
For Psyche's birth . . . And that is our death!

196

MY LADY'S LAW

The Law whereby my lady moves
Was never Law to me,
But 'tis enough that she approves
Whatever Law it be.

For in that Law, and by that Law,
My constant course I'll steer;
Not that I heed or deem it dread,
But that she holds it dear.

Tho' Asia sent for my content
Her richest argosies,
Those would I spurn, and bid return,
If that should give her ease.

With equal heart I'd watch depart
Each spicèd sail from sight,
Sans bitterness, desiring less
Great gear than her delight.

Though Kings made swift with many a gift
My proven sword to hire,
I would not go nor serve 'em so,
Except at her desire.

With even mind, I'd put behind
Adventure and acclaim,
And clean give o'er, esteeming more
Her favour than my fame.

Yet such am I, yea such am I—
Sore bond and freest free,
The Law that sways my lady's ways
Is mystery to me!

THE NURSING SISTER

(Maternity Hospital)

Our sister sayeth such and such.
And we must bow to her behests;
Our sister toileth overmuch,
Our little maid that hath no breasts.

A field untilled, a web unwove,
A flower withheld from sun or bee,
An alien in the courts of Love,
And—teacher unto such as we!

We love her, but we laugh the while,
We laugh, but sobs are mixed with laughter;
Our sister hath no time to smile,
She knows not what must follow after.

Wind of the South, arise and blow,
From beds of spice thy locks shake free;
Breathe on her heart that she may know,
Breathe on her eyes that she may see.

Alas! we vex her with our mirth,
And maze her with most tender scorn,
Who stands beside the gates of Birth,
Herself a child—a child unborn!

Our sister sayeth such and such,
And we must bow to her behests;
Our sister toileth overmuch,
Our little maid that hath no breasts.

THE LOVE SONG OF HAR DYAL

Alone upon the housetops to the North
I turn and watch the lightning in the sky—
The glamour of thy footsteps in the North.
Come back to me, Beloved, or I die.

Below my feet the still bazar is laid—
Far, far below the weary camels lie—
The camels and the captives of thy raid.
Come back to me, Beloved, or I die!

My father's wife is old and harsh with years,
And drudge of all my father's house am I—
My bread is sorrow and my drink is tears.
Come back to me. Beloved, or I die!

A DEDICATION

And they were stronger hands than mine
That digged the Ruby from the earth—
More cunning brains that made it worth
The large desire of a king,
And stouter hearts that through the brine
Went down the perfect Pearl to bring.

Lo, I have wrought in common clay
Rude figures of a rough-hewn race,
Since pearls strew not the market-place
In this my town of banishment,
Where with the shifting dust I play,
And eat the bread of discontent.

Yet is there life in that I make.
O thou who knowest, turn and see—
As thou hast power over me
So have I power over these,
Because I wrought them for thy sake,
And breathed in them mine agonies.

Small mirth was in the making—now
I lift the cloth that cloaks the clay,
And, wearied, at thy feet I lay
My wares, ere I go forth to sell.
The long bazar will praise, but thou—
Heart of my heart—have I done well?

MOTHER O' MINE

If I were hanged on the highest hill,
Mother o' mine, O mother o' mine!
I know whose love would follow me still,
Mother o' mine, O mother o' mine!

If I were drowned in the deepest sea,
Mother o' mine, O mother o' mine!
I know whose tears would come down to me,
Mother o' mine, O mother o' mine!

If I were damned of body and soul,
I know whose prayers would make me whole,
Mother o' mine, O mother o' mine!

THE ONLY SON

She dropped the bar, she shot the bolt, she fed the fire anew,
For she heard a whimper under the sill and a great grey paw came through.
The fresh flame comforted the hut and shone on the roof-beam,
And the Only Son lay down again and dreamed that he dreamed a dream.
The last ash fell from the withered log with the click of a falling spark,
And the Only Son woke up again, and called across the dark:—
'Now was I born of womankind and laid in a mother's breast?
For I have dreamed of a shaggy hide whereon I went to rest?
And was I born of womankind and laid on a father's arm?
For I have dreamed of clashing teeth that guarded me from harm.
And was I born an Only Son and did I play alone?
For I have dreamed of comrades twain that bit me to the bone.
And did I break the barley-cake and steep it in the tyre?
For I have dreamed of a youngling kid new-riven from the byre.
For I have dreamed of a midnight sky and a midnight call to blood,
And red-mouthed shadows racing by, that thrust me from my food.
'Tis an hour yet and an hour yet to the rising of the moon,
But I can see the black roof-tree as plain as it were noon.
'Tis a league and a league to the Lena Falls where the trooping blackbuck
    go;
But I can hear the little fawn that bleats behind the doe.
'Tis a league and a league to the Lena Falls where the crop and the upland
    meet,
But I can smell the wet dawn-wind that wakes the sprouting wheat.

Unbar the door, I may not bide, but I must out and see
If those are wolves that wait outside or my own kin to me!'

* * * * *

She loosed the bar, she slid the bolt, she opened the door anon,
And a grey bitch-wolf came out of the dark and fawned on the Only
    Son!

MOWGLI'S SONG AGAINST PEOPLE

I will let loose against you the fleet-footed vines—
I will call in the Jungle to stamp out your lines!
    The roofs shall fade before it,
      The house-beams shall fall,
  And the *Karela*, the bitter *Karela*,
    Shall cover it all!

In the gates of these your councils my people shall sing,
In the doors of these your garners the Bat-folk shall cling;
    And the snake shall be your watchman,
      By a hearthstone unswept;
  For the *Karela*, the bitter *Karela*,
    Shall fruit where ye slept!

Ye shall not see my strikers; ye shall hear them and guess;
By night, before the moon-rise, I will send for my cess,
    And the wolf shall be your herdsman
      By a landmark removed,
  For the *Karela*, the bitter *Karela*,
    Shall seed where ye loved!

I will reap your fields before you at the hands of a host;
Ye shall glean behind my reapers for the bread that is lost;
    And the deer shall be your oxen
      On a headland untilled,

For the *Karela*, the bitter *Karela*,
    Shall leaf where ye build!

I have untied against you the club-footed vines—
I have sent in the Jungle to swamp out your lines!
    The trees—the trees are on you!
      The house-beams shall fall,
    And the *Karela*, the bitter *Karela*,
      Shall cover you all!

ROMULUS AND REMUS

Oh, little did the Wolf-Child care,
    When first he planned his home,
What City should arise and bear
    The weight and state of Rome!

A shiftless, westward-wandering tramp,
    Checked by the Tiber flood,
He reared a wall around his camp
    Of uninspired mud.

But when his brother leaped the Wall
    And mocked its height and make,
He guessed the future of it all
    And slew him for its sake.

Swift was the blow—swift as the thought
    Which showed him in that hour
How unbelief may bring to naught
    The early steps of Power.

Foreseeing Time's imperilled hopes
    Of Glory, Grace, and Love—
All singers, Cæsars, artists, Popes—
    Would fail if Remus throve,

He sent his brother to the Gods,
　　And, when the fit was o'er,
Went on collecting turves and clods
　　To build the Wall once more!

CHAPTER HEADINGS

THE JUNGLE BOOKS

Now Chil the Kite brings home the night
    That Mang the Bat sets free—
The herds are shut in byre and hut
    For loosed till dawn are we.
This is the hour of pride and power,
    Talon and tush and claw.
Oh hear the call!—Good hunting all
    That keep the Jungle Law!

    Mowgli's Brothers.

* * * * *

His spots are the joy of the Leopard: his horns are the Buffalo's pride.
Be clean, for the strength of the hunter is known by the gloss of his hide.
If ye find that the bullock can toss you, or the heavy-browed Sambhur
    can gore;
Ye need not stop work to inform us. We knew it ten seasons before.
Oppress not the cubs of the stranger, but hail them as Sister and Brother,
For though they are little and fubsy, it may be the Bear is their mother.
'There is none like to me!' says the Cub in the pride of his earliest kill;
But the Jungle is large and the Cub he is small. Let him think and be still.

    Kaa's Hunting.

* * * * *

The stream is shrunk—the pool is dry,
And we be comrades, thou and I;
With fevered jowl and dusty flank
Each jostling each along the bank;
And, by one drouthy fear made still,
Foregoing thought of quest or kill.
Now 'neath his dam the fawn may see,
The lean Pack-wolf as cowed as he,
And the tall buck, unflinching, note
The fangs that tore his father's throat.
The pools are shrunk—the streams are dry,
And we be playmates, thou and I,
Till yonder cloud—Good Hunting!—loose
The rain that breaks our Water Truce.

How Fear Came.

* * * * *

What of the hunting, hunter bold?
    Brother, the watch was long and cold.
What of the quarry ye went to kill?
    Brother, he crops in the jungle still.
Where is the power that made your pride?
    Brother, it ebbs from my flank and side.
Where is the haste that ye hurry by?
    Brother, I go to my lair to die!

'Tiger-Tiger!'

* * * * *

Veil them, cover them, wall them round—
    Blossom, and creeper, and weed—
Let us forget the sight and the sound,
    The smell and the touch of the breed!

Fat black ash by the altar-stone.
    Here is the white-foot rain,
And the does bring forth in the fields unsown,
    And none shall affright them again;
And the blind walls crumble, unknown, o'erthrown,
    And none shall inhabit again!

     Letting in the Jungle.

* * * * *

These are the Four that are never content, that have never been filled
    since the Dews began—
Jacala's mouth, and the glut of the Kite, and the hands of the Ape, and
    the Eyes of Man.

     The King's Ankus.

* * * * *

For our white and our excellent nights—for the nights of swift running,
    Fair ranging, far-seeing, good hunting, sure cunning!
For the smells of the dawning, untainted, ere dew has departed!
For the rush through the mist, and the quarry blind-started!
For the cry of our mates when the sambhur has wheeled and is standing
    at bay!
            For the risk and the riot of night!
            For the sleep at the lair-mouth by day!

It is met, and we go to the fight.
Bay! O bay!

Red Dog.

* * * * *

Man goes to Man! Cry the challenge through the Jungle!
    He that was our Brother goes away.
Hear, now, and judge, O ye People of the Jungle,—
    Answer, who shall turn him—who shall stay?

Man goes to Man! He is weeping in the Jungle:
    He that was our Brother sorrows sore!
Man goes to Man! (Oh, we loved him in the Jungle!)
    To the Man-Trail where we may not follow more.

The Spring Running.

* * * * *

At the hole where he went in
Red-Eye called to Wrinkle-Skin.
Hear what little Red-Eye saith:
'Nag, come up and dance with death!'

Eye to eye and head to head,
    (Keep the measure, Nag.)
This shall end when one is dead;
    (At thy pleasure, Nag.)

Turn for turn and twist for twist—
    (Run and hide thee, Nag.)

Hah! The hooded Death has missed!
(Woe betide thee, Nag!)

    'Rikki-Tikki-Tavi.'

* * * * *

Oh! hush thee, my baby, the night is behind us,
    And black are the waters that sparkled so green.
The moon, o'er the combers, looks downward to find us
    At rest in the hollows that rustle between.
Where billow meets billow, there soft be thy pillow;
    Ah, weary wee flipperling, curl at thy ease!
The storm shall not wake thee, nor shark overtake thee,
    Asleep in the arms of the slow-swinging seas.

    The White Seal.

* * * * *

You mustn't swim till you're six weeks old,
    Or your head will be sunk by your heels;
And summer gales and Killer Whales
    Are bad for baby seals.
Are bad for baby seals, dear rat,
    As bad as bad can be;
But splash and grow strong,
And you can't be wrong,
    Child of the Open Sea!

    The White Seal.

* * * * *

215

I will remember what I was, I am sick of rope and chain.
    I will remember my old strength and all my forest affairs.
I will not sell my back to man for a bundle of sugar-cane.
    I will go out to my own kind, and the wood-folk in their lairs.

I will go out until the day, until the morning break,
    Out to the winds' untainted kiss, the waters' clean caress.
I will forget my ankle-ring and snap my picket-stake.
    I will revisit my lost loves, and playmates master-less!

    Toomai of the Elephants.

∗ ∗ ∗ ∗ ∗

The People of the Eastern Ice, they are melting like the snow—
They beg for coffee and sugar; they go where the white men go.
The People of the Western Ice, they learn to steal and fight;
They sell their furs to the trading-post; they sell their souls to the white.
The People of the Southern Ice, they trade with the whaler's crew;
Their women have many ribbons, but their tents are torn and few.
But the People of the Elder Ice, beyond the white man's ken—
Their spears are made of the narwhal-horn, and they are the last of the
    Men!

    Quiquern.

∗ ∗ ∗ ∗ ∗

When ye say to Tabaqui, 'My Brother!' when ye call the Hyena to meat,
Ye may cry the Full Truce with Jacala—the Belly that runs on four feet.

    The Undertakers.

* * * * *

The night we felt the earth would move
    We stole and plucked him by the hand,
Because we loved him with the love
    That knows but cannot understand.

And when the roaring hillside broke,
    And all our world fell down in rain,
We saved him, we the Little Folk;
    But lo! he does not come again!

Mourn now, we saved him for the sake
    Of such poor love as wild ones may.
Mourn ye! Our brother will not wake,
    And his own kind drive us away!

The Miracle of Purun Bhagat.

THE EGG-SHELL

The wind took off with the sunset—
The fog came up with the tide,
When the Witch of the North took an Egg-shell
With a little Blue Devil inside.
'Sink,' she said, 'or swim,' she said,
'It's all you will get from me.
And that is the finish of *him*!' she said.
And the Egg-shell went to sea.

The wind fell dead with the midnight—
The fog shut down like a sheet,
When the Witch of the North heard the Egg-shell
Feeling by hand for a fleet.
'Get!' she said, 'or you're gone,' she said,
But the little Blue Devil said 'No!'
'The sights are just coming on,' he said,
And he let the Whitehead go.

The wind got up with the morning—
And the fog blew off with the rain,
When the Witch of the North saw the Egg-shell
And the little Blue Devil again.
'Did you swim?' she said. 'Did you sink?' she said,
And the little Blue Devil replied:
'For myself I swam, but I think,' he said,
'There's somebody sinking outside.'

218

THE KING'S TASK

After the sack of the City, when Rome was sunk to a name,
In the years that the lights were darkened, or ever St. Wilfrid came,
Low on the borders of Britain (the ancient poets sing)
Between the Cliff and the Forest there ruled a Saxon King.
Stubborn all were his people from cottar to overlord—
Not to be cowed by the cudgel, scarce to be schooled by the sword;
Quick to turn at their pleasure, cruel to cross in their mood,
And set on paths of their choosing as the hogs of Andred's Wood.
Laws they made in the Witan—the laws of flaying and fine—
Common, loppage and pannage, the theft and the track of kine—
Statutes of tun and market for the fish and the malt and the meal—
The tax on the Bramber packhorse and the tax on the Hastings keel.
Over the graves of the Druids and under the wreck of Rome
Rudely but surely they bedded the plinth of the days to come.
Behind the feet of the Legions and before the Norseman's ire,
Rudely but greatly begat they the framing of state and shire.
Rudely but deeply they laboured, and their labour stands till now,
If we trace on our ancient headlands the twist of their eight-ox plough.
There came a king from Hamtun, by Bosenham he came.
He filled Use with slaughter, and Lewes he gave to flame.
He smote while they sat in the Witan—sudden he smote and sore,
That his fleet was gathered at Selsea ere they mustered at Cymen's Ore.
Blithe went the Saxons to battle, by down and wood and mere,
But thrice the acorns ripened ere the western mark was clear.
Thrice was the beechmast gathered, and the Beltane fires burned

Thrice, and the beeves were salted thrice ere the host returned.
They drove that king from Hamtun, by Bosenham o'erthrown,
Out of Rugnor to Wilton they made his land their own.
Camps they builded at Gilling, at Basing and Alresford,
But wrath abode in the Saxons from cottar to overlord.
Wrath at the weary war-game, at the foe that snapped and ran
Wolf-wise feigning and flying, and wolf-wise snatching his man.
Wrath for their spears unready, their levies new to the blades—
Shame for the helpless sieges and the scornful ambuscades.
At hearth and tavern and market, wherever the tale was told,
Shame and wrath had the Saxons because of their boasts of old.
And some would drink and deny it, and some would pray and atone;
But the most part, after their anger, avouched that the sin was their
    own.
Wherefore, girding together, up to the Witan they came,
And as they had shouldered their bucklers so did they shoulder their
    blame.
For that was the wont of the Saxons (the ancient poets sing),
And first they spoke in the Witan and then they spoke to the King:
'Edward King of the Saxons, thou knowest from sire to son,
'One is the King and his People—in gain and ungain one.
'Count we the gain together. With doubtings and spread dismays
'We have broken a foolish people—but after many days.
'Count we the loss together. Warlocks hampered our arms,
'We were tricked as by magic, we were turned as by charms.
'We went down to the battle and the road was plain to keep,
'But our angry eyes were holden, and we struck as they strike in sleep—
'Men new shaken from slumber, sweating, with eyes a-stare
'Little blows uncertain dealt on the useless air.
'Also a vision betrayed us, and a lying tale made bold
'That we looked to hold what we had not and to have what we did not
    hold:

220

'That a shield should give us shelter—that a sword should give us
   power—
'A shield snatched up at a venture and a hilt scarce handled an hour:
'That being rich in the open, we should be strong in the close—
'And the Gods would sell us a cunning for the day that we met our foes.
'This was the work of wizards, but not with our foe they bide,
'In our own camp we took them, and their names are Sloth and Pride.
'Our pride was before the battle: our sloth ere we lifted spear,
'But hid in the heart of the people as the fever hides in the mere,
'Waiting only the war-game, the heat of the strife to rise
'As the ague fumes round Oxeney when the rotting reed-bed dries.
'But now we are purged of that fever—cleansed by the letting of blood,
'Something leaner of body—something keener of mood.
'And the men new-freed from the levies return to the fields again,
'Matching a hundred battles, cottar and lord and thane.
'And they talk aloud in the temples where the ancient wargods are.
'They thumb and mock and belittle the holy harness of war.
'They jest at the sacred chariots, the robes and the gilded staff.
'These things fill them with laughter, they lean on their spears and
   laugh.
'The men grown old in the war-game, hither and thither they range—
'And scorn and laughter together are sire and dam of change;
'And change may be good or evil—but we know not what it will bring,
'Therefore our King must teach us. That is thy task, O King!'

POSEIDON'S LAW

When the robust and Brass-bound Man commissioned first for sea
His fragile raft, Poseidon laughed, and 'Mariner,' said he,
'Behold, a Law immutable I lay on thee and thine,
That never shall ye act or tell a falsehood at my shrine.

'Let Zeus adjudge your landward kin, whose votive meal and salt
At easy-cheated altars win oblivion for the fault,
But you the unhoodwinked wave shall test—the immediate gulf
    condemn—
Except ye owe the Fates a jest, be slow to jest with them.

'Ye shall not clear by Greekly speech, nor cozen from your path
The twinkling shoal, the leeward beach, and Hadria's white-lipped wrath;
Nor tempt with painted cloth for wood my fraud-avenging hosts;
Nor make at all, or all make good, your bulwarks and your boasts.

'Now and henceforward serve unshod, through wet and wakeful shifts,
A present and oppressive God, but take, to aid, my gifts—
The wide and windward-opening eye, the large and lavish hand,
The soul that cannot tell a lie—except upon the land!'

In dromond and in catafract—wet, wakeful, windward-eyed—
He kept Poseidon's Law intact (his ship and freight beside),
But, once discharged the dromond's hold, the bireme beached once more,
Splendaciously mendacious rolled the Brass-bound Man ashore.

The thranite now and thalamite are pressures low and high,
And where three hundred blades bit white the twin-propellers ply:
The God that hailed, the keel that sailed, are changed beyond recall,
But the robust and Brass-bound Man he is not changed at all!

From Punt returned, from Phormio's Fleet, from Javan and Gadire,
He strongly occupies the seat about the tavern fire,
And, moist with much Falernian or smoked Massilian juice,
Revenges there the Brass-bound Man his long-enforced truce!

A TRUTHFUL SONG

The Bricklayer:

I tell this tale, which is strictly true,
Just by way of convincing you
How very little, since things were made,
Things have altered in the building trade.

A year ago, come the middle of March,
We was building flats near the Marble Arch,
When a thin young man with coal-black hair
Came up to watch us working there.

Now there wasn't a trick in brick or stone
That this young man hadn't seen or known;
Nor there wasn't a tool from trowel to maul
But this young man could use 'em all!

Then up and spoke the plumbyers bold,
Which was laying the pipes for the hot and cold:
'Since you with us have made so free,
Will you kindly say what your name might be?'

The young man kindly answered them:
'It might be Lot or Methusalem,
Or it might be Moses (a man I hate),
Whereas it is Pharaoh surnamed the Great.

'Your glazing is new and your plumbing's strange,
But otherwise I perceive no change,
And in less than a month if you do as I bid
I'd learn you to build me a Pyramid!'

The Sailor:

I tell this tale, which is stricter true,
Just by way of convincing you
How very little, since things was made,
Things have altered in the shipwright's trade.

In Blackwall Basin yesterday
A China barque re-fitting lay,
When a fat old man with snow-white hair
Came up to watch us working there.

Now there wasn't a knot which the riggers knew
But the old man made it—and better too;
Nor there wasn't a sheet, or a lift, or a brace,
But the old man knew its lead and place.

Then up and spoke the caulkyers bold,
Which was packing the pump in the afterhold:
'Since you with us have made so free,
Will you kindly tell what your name might be?'

The old man kindly answered them:
'It might be Japheth, it might be Shem,
Or it might be Ham (though his skin was dark),
Whereas it is Noah, commanding the Ark.

'Your wheel is new and your pumps are strange,
But otherwise I perceive no change,
And in less than a week, if she did not ground,
I'd sail this hooker the wide world round!'

Both:

We tell these tales, which are strictest true,
Just by way of convincing you
How very little, since things was made,
Anything alters in any one's trade.

A SMUGGLER'S SONG

If you wake at midnight, and hear a horse's feet,
Don't go drawing back the blind, or looking in the street.
Them that asks no questions isn't told a lie,
Watch the wall, my darling, while the Gentlemen go by!
      Five and twenty ponies,
      Trotting through the dark—
      Brandy for the Parson,
      'Baccy for the Clerk;
      Laces for a lady, letters for a spy,
And watch the wall, my darling, while the Gentlemen go by!

Running round the woodlump if you chance to find
Little barrels, roped and tarred, all full of brandy-wine,
Don't you shout to come and look, nor use 'em for your play.
Put the brishwood back again—and they'll be gone next day!

If you see the stable-door setting open wide;
If you see a tired horse lying down inside;
If your mother mends a coat cut about and tore;
If the lining's wet and warm—don't you ask no more!

If you meet King George's men, dressed in blue and red,
You be careful what you say, and mindful what is said.
If they call you 'pretty maid,' and chuck you 'neath the chin.
Don't you tell where no one is, nor yet where no one's been!

Knocks and footsteps round the house—whistles after dark—
You've no call for running out till the house-dogs bark.
Trusty's here, and *Pinchers* here, and see how dumb they lie—
They don't fret to follow when the Gentlemen go by!

If you do as you've been told, 'likely there's a chance,
You'll be give a dainty doll, all the way from France,
With a cap of Valenciennes, and a velvet hood—
A present from the Gentlemen, along o' being good!
      Five and twenty ponies,
      Trotting through the dark—
      Brandy for the Parson,
      'Baccy for the Clerk.
Them that asks no questions isn't told a lie—
Watch the wall, my darling, while the Gentlemen go by!

228

KING HENRY VII. AND THE SHIPWRIGHTS

(A.D. 1487)

Harry, our King in England, from London town is gone,
And comen to Hamull on the Hoke in the countie of Suthampton.
For there lay *The Mary of the Tower*, his ship of war so strong,
And he would discover, certaynely, if his shipwrights did him wrong.

He told not none of his setting forth, nor yet where he would go
(But only my Lord of Arundel), and meanly did he show,
In an old jerkin and patched hose that no man might him mark;
With his frieze hood and cloak above, he looked like any clerk.

He was at Hamull on the Hoke about the hour of the tide.
And saw the *Mary* haled into dock, the winter to abide,
With all her tackle and habiliments which are the King his own;
But then ran on his false shipwrights and stripped her to the bone.

They heaved the main-mast overboard, that was of a trusty tree,
And they wrote down it was spent and lost by force of weather at sea.
But they sawen it into planks and strakes as far as it might go,
To maken beds for their own wives and little children also.

There was a knave called Slingawai, he crope beneath the deck.
Crying: 'Good felawes, come and see! The ship is nigh a wreck!
For the storm that took our tall main-mast, it blew so fierce and fell,
Alack! it hath taken the kettles and pans, and this brass pott as well!'

With that he set the pott on his head and hied him up the hatch,
While all the shipwrights ran below to find what they might snatch;
All except Bob Brygandyne and he was a yeoman good,
He caught Slingawai round the waist and threw him on to the mud.

'I have taken plank and rope and nail, without the King his leave,
After the custom of Portesmouth, but I will not suffer a thief.
Nay, never lift up thy hand at me! There's no clean hands in the trade—
Steal in measure,' quo' Brygandyne. 'There's measure in all things made!'

'Gramercy, yeoman!' said our King. 'Thy council liketh me.'
And he pulled a whistle out of his neck and whistled whistles three.
Then came my Lord of Arundel pricking across the down,
And behind him the Mayor and Burgesses of merry Suthampton town.

They drew the naughty shipwrights up, with the kettles in their hands,
And bound them round the forecastle to wait the King's commands.
But 'Since ye have made your beds,' said the King, 'ye needs must lie
     thereon.
For the sake of your wives and little ones—felawes, get you gone!'

When they had beaten Slingawai, out of his own lips
Our King appointed Brygandyne to be Clerk of all his ships.
'Nay, never lift up thy hands to me—there's no clean hands in the trade.
But steal in measure,' said Harry our King. 'There's measure in all things
     made!'

God speed the 'Mary of the Tower,' the 'Sovereign,' and 'Grace Dieu,'
The 'Sweepstakes' and the 'Mary Fortune,' and the 'Henry of Bristol' too!
All tall ships that sail on, the sea, or in our harbours stand,
That they may keep measure with Harry our King and peace in Engeland!

THE WET LITANY

When the water's countenance
Blurrs 'twixt glance and second glance;
When our tattered smokes forerun.
Ashen 'neath a silvered sun;
When the curtain of the haze
Shuts upon our helpless ways—
    Hear the Channel Fleet at sea;
    Libera nos Domine!

When the engines' bated pulse
Scarcely thrills the nosing hulls;
When the wash along the side
Sounds, a sudden, magnified;
When the intolerable blast
Marks each blindfold minute passed;

When the fog-buoy's squattering flight
Guides us through the haggard night;
When the warning bugle blows;
When the lettered doorways close;
When our brittle townships press,
Impotent, on emptiness;

When the unseen leadsmen lean
Questioning a deep unseen;

When their lessened count they tell
To a bridge invisible;
When the hid and perilous
Cliffs return our cry to us;

When the treble thickness spread
Swallows up our next-ahead;
When her siren's frightened whine
Shows her sheering out of line;
When, her passage undiscerned,
We must turn where she has turned,
    Hear the Channel Fleet at sea:
    Libera nos Domine!

THE BALLAD OF MINEPIT SHAW

About the time that taverns shut
    And men can buy no beer,
Two lads went up to the keepers' hut
    To steal Lord Pelham's deer.

Night and the liquor was in their heads—
    They laughed and talked no bounds,
Till they waked the keepers on their beds,
    And the keepers loosed the hounds.

They had killed a hart, they had killed a hind,
    Ready to carry away,
When they heard a whimper down the wind
    And they heard a bloodhound bay.

They took and ran across the fern,
    Their crossbows in their hand,
Till they met a man with a green lantern
    That called and bade 'em stand.

'What are ye doing, O Flesh and Blood,
    And what's your foolish will,
That you must break into Minepit Wood
    And wake the Folk of the Hill?'

'Oh, we've broke into Lord Pelham's park,
 And killed Lord Pelham's deer,
And if ever you heard a little dog bark
 You'll know why we come here.

'We ask you let us go our way,
 As fast as we can flee,
For if ever you heard a bloodhound bay
 You'll know how pressed we be.'

'Oh, lay your crossbows on the bank
 And drop the knife from your hand,
And though the hounds are at your flank
 I'll save you where you stand!'

They laid their crossbows on the bank,
 They threw their knives in the wood,
And the ground before them opened and sank
 And saved 'em where they stood.

'Oh, what's the roaring in our ears
 That strikes us well-nigh dumb?'
'Oh, that is just how things appears
 According as they come.'

'What are the stars before our eyes
 That strike us well-nigh blind?'
'Oh, that is just how things arise
 According as you find.'

'And why's our bed so hard to the bones
 Excepting where it's cold?'

234

'Oh, that's because it is precious stones
    Excepting where 'tis gold.

'Think it over as you stand.
    For I tell you without fail,
If you haven't got into Fairyland
    You're not in Lewes Gaol.'

All night long they thought of it,
    And, come the dawn, they saw
They'd tumbled into a great old pit,
    At the bottom of Minepit Shaw.

And the keepers' hound had followed 'em close,
    And broke her neck in the fall;
So they picked up their knives and their crossbows
    And buried the dog. That's all.

But whether the man was a poacher too
    Or a Pharisee[2] so bold—
I reckon there's more things told than are true,
    And more things true than are told!

---

2 A fairy.

HERIOT'S FORD

'What's that that hirples at my side?'
The foe that you must fight, my lord.
'That rides as fast as I can ride?'
The shadow of your might, my lord.

'Then wheel my horse against the foe!'
He's down and overpast, my lord.
You war against the sunset glow,
The judgment follows fast, my lord.

'Oh who will stay the sun's descent?'
King Joshua he is dead, my lord.
'I need an hour to repent!'
'Tis what our sister said, my lord.

'Oh do not slay me in my sins!'
You're safe awhile with us, my lord.
'Nay, kill me ere my fear begins.'
We would not serve you thus, my lord.

'Where is the doom that I must face?'
Three little leagues away, my lord.
'Then mend the horses' laggard pace!'
We need them for next day, my lord.

'Next day—next day! Unloose my cords!'
Our sister needed none, my lord.
You had no mind to face our swords,
And—where can cowards run, my lord?

'You would not kill the soul alive?'
'Twas thus our sister cried, my lord.
'I dare not die with none to shrive.'
But so our sister died, my lord.

'Then wipe the sweat from brow and cheek.
It runnels forth afresh, my lord.
'Uphold me—for the flesh is weak.'
You've finished with the Flesh, my lord.

FRANKIE'S TRADE

Old Horn to All Atlantic said:
    (A-hay O! To me O!')
'Now where did Frankie learn his trade?
For he ran me down with a three-reef mains'le.'
    (All round the Horn!)

Atlantic answered:—'Not from me!
You'd better ask the cold North Sea,
For he ran me down under all plain canvas.'
    (All round the Horn!)

The North Sea answered:—'He's my man,
For he came to me when he began—
Frankie Drake in an open coaster.
    (All round the Sands!)

'I caught him young and I used him sore,
So you never shall startle Frankie more,
Without capsizing Earth and her waters.
    (All round the Sands!)

'I did not favour him at all.
I made him pull and I made him haul—
And stand his trick with the common sailors.
    (All round the Sands!)

'I froze him stiff and I fogged him blind.
And kicked him home with his road to find
By what he could see in a three-day snow-storm
    (All round the Sands!)

'I learned him his trade o' winter nights,
'Twixt Mardyk Fort and Dunkirk lights
On a five-knot tide with the forts a-firing.
    (All round the Sands!)

'Before his beard began to shoot,
I showed him the length of the Spaniard's foot—
And I reckon he clapped the boot on it later.
    (All round the Sands!)

'If there's a risk which you can make.
That's worse than he was used to take
Nigh every week in the way of his business;
    (All round the Sands!)

'If there's a trick that you can try,
Which he hasn't met in time gone by,
Not once or twice, but ten times over;
    (All round the Sands!)

'If you can teach him aught that's new,
    (A-hay O! To me O!)
I'll give you Bruges and Niewport too,
And the ten tall churches that stand between 'em.'
    Storm along my gallant Captains!
    (All round the Horn!)

THE JUGGLER'S SONG

When the drums begin to beat
Down the street,
When the poles are fetched and guyed,
When the tight-rope's stretched and tied,
When the dance-girls make salaam,
When the snake-bag wakes alarm,
When the pipes set up their drone,
When the sharp-edged knives are thrown,
When the red-hot coals are shown,
To be swallowed by and bye—
Arré Brethren, here come I!

Stripped to loin-cloth in the sun,
Search me well and watch me close!
Tell me how my tricks are done—
Tell me how the mango grows?
Give a man who is not made
To his trade
Swords to fling and catch again,
Coins to ring and snatch again,
Men to harm and cure again.
Snakes to charm and lure again—
He'll be hurt by his own blade,
By his serpents disobeyed,
By his clumsiness bewrayed,

By the people laughed to scorn—
So 'tis not with juggler born!

Pinch of dust or withered flower,
Chance-flung nut or borrowed staff,
Serve his need and shore his power,
Bind the spell or loose the laugh!

THORKILD'S SONG

There's no wind along these seas.
Out oars for Stavanger!
Forward all for Stavanger!
So we must wake the white-ash breeze,
Let fall for Stavanger!
A long pull for Stavanger!

Oh, hear the benches creak and strain!
(A long pull for Stavanger!)
She thinks she smells the Northland rain!
(A long pull for Stavanger!)

She thinks she smells the Northland snow,
And she's as glad as we to go.

She thinks she smells the Northland rime,
And the dear dark nights of winter-time.

She wants to be at her own home pier,
To shift her sails and standing gear.

She wants to be in her winter-shed.
To strip herself and go to bed.

Her very bolts are sick for shore,
And we—we want it ten times more!

So all you Gods that love brave men,
Send us a three-reef gale again!

Send us a gale, and watch us come,
With close-cropped canvas slashing home!

But—there's no wind on all these seas,
A long pull for Stavanger!
So we must wake the white-ash breeze,
A long pull for Stavanger!

'ANGUTIVAUN TAINA'

Song of the Returning Hunter (Esquimaux).

Our gloves are stiff with the frozen blood,
    Our furs with the drifted snow,
As we come in with the seal—the seal!
    In from the edge of the floe.

An jana! Aua! Oha! Haq!
    And the yelping dog-teams go,
And the long whips crack, and the men come back,
    Back from the edge of the floe!

We tracked our seal to his secret place,
    We heard him scratch below,
We made our mark, and we watched beside,
    Out on the edge of the floe.

We raised our lance when he rose to breathe,
    We drove it downward—so!
And we played him thus, and we killed him thus,
    Out on the edge of the floe.

Our gloves are glued with the frozen blood,
    Our eyes with the drifting snow;

244

But we come back to our wives again,
  Back from the edge of the floe!

Au jana! Aua! Oha! Haq!
  And the loaded dog-teams go,
And the wives can hear their men come back,
  Back from the edge of the floe!

HUNTING-SONG OF
THE SEEONEE PACK

As the dawn was breaking the Sambhur belled—
    Once, twice and again!
And a doe leaped up, and a doe leaped up
From the pond in the wood where the wild deer sup.
This I, scouting alone, beheld,
    Once, twice and again!

As the dawn was breaking the Sambhur belled—
    Once, twice and again!
And a wolf stole back, and a wolf stole back
To carry the word to the waiting pack,
And we sought and we found and we bayed on his track
    Once, twice and again!

As the dawn was breaking the Wolf Pack yelled
    Once, twice and again!
Feet in the jungle that leave no mark!
Eyes that can see in the dark—the dark!
Tongue—give tongue to it! Hark! O hark!
    Once, twice and again!

SONG OF THE MEN'S SIDE

(Neolithic)

Once we feared The Beast—when he followed us we ran,
    Ran very fast though we knew
It was not right that The Beast should master Man;
    But what could we Flint-workers do?
The Beast only grinned at our spears round his ears—
    Grinned at the hammers that we made;
But now we will hunt him for the life with the Knife—
    And this is the Buyer of the Blade!

> *Room for his shadow on the grass—let it pass!*
>   *To left and right—stand clear!*
> *This is the Buyer of the Blade—be afraid!*
>   *This is the great god Tyr!*

Tyr thought hard till he hammered out a plan,
    For he knew it was not right
(And it *is* not right) that The Beast should master Man;
    So he went to the Children of the Night.
He begged a Magic Knife of their make for our sake.
    When he begged for the Knife they said:
'The price of the Knife you would buy is an eye!'
    And that was the price he paid.

Tell it to the Barrows of the Dead—run ahead!
Shout it so the Women's Side can hear!
This is the Buyer of the Blade—be afraid!
This is the great god Tyr!

Our women and our little ones may walk on the Chalk,
    As far as we can see them and beyond.
We shall not be anxious for our sheep when we keep
    Tally at the shearing-pond.
We can eat with both our elbows on our knees, if we please,
    We can sleep after meals in the sun;
For Shepherd of the Twilight is dismayed at the Blade,
    Feet-in-the-Night have run!
Dog-without-a-Master goes away (Hai, Tyr, aie!),
    Devil-in-the-Dusk has run!

Then:

Room for his shadow on the grass—let it pass!
To left and right—stand clear!
This is the Buyer of the Blade—be afraid!
This is the great god Tyr!

DARZEE'S CHAUNT

(Sung in honour of Rikki-tikki-tavi)

Singer and tailor am I—
    Doubled the joys that I know—
Proud of my lilt to the sky,
    Proud of the house that I sew—
Over and under, so weave I my music—so weave I the house that I sew.

Sing to your fledglings again,
    Mother, O lift up your head!
Evil that plagued us is slain,
    Death in the garden lies dead.
Terror that hid in the roses is impotent—flung on the dung-hill and dead!

Who hath delivered us, who?
    Tell me his nest and his name.
Rikki, the valiant, the true,
    Tikki, with eyeballs of flame,
Rik-tikki-tikki, the ivory-fanged, the hunter with eyeballs of flame.

Give him the Thanks of the Birds,
Bowing with tail-feathers spread!
Praise him with nightingale-words—
Nay, I will praise him instead.
Hear! I will sing you the praise of the bottle-tailed Rikki, with eyeballs
of red!

(Here Rikki-tikki interrupted, and the rest of the song is lost.)

THE FOUR ANGELS

As Adam lay a-dreaming beneath the Apple Tree,
The Angel of the Earth came down, and offered Earth in fee.
        But Adam did not need it,
           Nor the plough he would not speed it,
   Singing:—'Earth and Water, Air and Fire,
            What more can mortal man desire?'
           (The Apple Tree's in bud.)

As Adam lay a-dreaming beneath the Apple Tree,
The Angel of the Waters offered all the Seas in fee.
        But Adam would not take 'em,
           Nor the ships he wouldn't make 'em,
   Singing:—'Water, Earth and Air and Fire,
            What more can mortal man desire?'
           (The Apple Tree's in leaf.)

As Adam lay a-dreaming beneath the Apple Tree,
The Angel of the Air he offered all the Air in fee.
        But Adam did not crave it,
           Nor the flight he wouldn't brave it,
   Singing:—'Air and Water, Earth and Fire,
            What more can mortal man desire?'
           (The Apple Tree's in bloom.)

As Adam lay a-dreaming beneath the Apple Tree,
The Angel of the Fire rose up and not a word said he,
 But he wished a flame and made it,
 And in Adam's heart he laid it,
 Singing:—'Fire, Fire, burning Fire!
 Stand up and reach your heart's desire!'
 (The Apple Blossom's set.)

As Adam was a-working outside of Eden-Wall,
He used the Earth, he used the Seas, he used the Air and all;
 And out of black disaster
 He arose to be the master
 Of Earth and Water, Air and Fire,
 But never reached his heart's desire!
 (The Apple Tree's cut down!)

THE PRAYER

My Brother kneels, so saith Kabir,
To stone and brass in heathen-wise,
But in my brother's voice I hear
My own unanswered agonies.
His God is as his fates assign,
His prayer is all the world's—and mine.

Lightning Source UK Ltd.
Milton Keynes UK
UKHW020016100223
416721UK00002B/420